BRITANNIA OBSCURA

ALSO BY JOANNE PARKER

England's Darling: The Victorian Cult of Alfred the Great

Britannia Obscura

Mapping Hidden Britain

JOANNE PARKER

JONATHAN CAPE
LONDON

Published by Jonathan Cape 2014

2 4 6 8 10 9 7 5 3 1

First published in Great Britain in 2014 by
Jonathan Cape
Random House, 20 Vauxhall Bridge Road,
London SW1V 2SA

www.vintage-books.co.uk

Addresses for companies within The Random House Group Limited can be found at:
www.randomhouse.co.uk/offices.htm

The Random House Group Limited Reg. No. 954009

A CIP catalogue record for this book is available from the British Library

ISBN 9780224102025

The Random House Group Limited supports the Forest Stewardship Council® (FSC®),
the leading international forest-certification organisation. Our books carrying the FSC label
are printed on FSC®-certified paper. FSC is the only forest-certification scheme supported by
the leading environmental organisations, including Greenpeace. Our paper procurement
policy can be found at www.randomhouse.co.uk/environment

Typeset in Dante MT by Palimpsest Book Production Ltd, Falkirk, Stirlingshire

Printed and bound in Great Britain by Clays Ltd, St Ives PLC

For Rosemary and Leonard Parker, and for Nick Groom.

Contents

List of Illustrations

'Lost Johns' Cave, Leck Fell. Leeds Cave Club Meet Easter 1932'. (Photographer: H.W. Haywood. Reproduced courtesy of the British Geological Survey CP14/067)

'Katie in the Trenches'. (Photographer: Rob Eavis. Reproduced courtesy of Rob Eavis)

'Katie Eavis in Titan'. (Photographer: Rob Eavis. Reproduced courtesy of Rob Eavis)

'A Scenographic View of the Druid Temple of Abury in North Wiltshire, As in its Original', by William Stukeley, from *Abury: A Temple of the British Druids* (London, 1743). (Reproduced courtesy of Special Collections, University of Exeter)

'Rollright Stones, Equinox'. (Photographer: Stefon Cox. Reproduced courtesy of Stefon Cox)

'Sea Pound, Glamorganshire Canal, Cardiff, 1921'. (Photographer: Aerofilms Ltd. Reproduced courtesy of the Royal Commission on the Ancient and Historical Monuments of Wales)

'Glamorganshire Canal, c.1977–8'. (Photographer: David Tromans. Reproduced courtesy of David Tromans and the Pontypridd Canal Conservation Group)

'Stalybridge'. (Photographer: Martin Clarke. Reproduced courtesy of Martin Clarke and The Horseboating Society)

'Map of Eight Leys Through Capel-Y-Tair-Ywen, Hay', by Alfred Watkins, in *Early British Trackways* (1922). (Reproduced courtesy of Exeter University Library)

'Members make for Pont Hendre'. (Reproduced courtesy of Herefordshire Museums Service)

'John Christian dowsing at Scorhill Circle, Gidleigh Common'. (Photographer: Chris Chapman. Reproduced courtesy of Chris Chapman)

'An exact representation of Mr Lunardi's New Balloon as it ascended with himself, 13 May 1785'. Mezzotint (London: Carrington Bowles, 1785). (Reproduced courtesy of the British Library)

'Samuel Cody, Cody 2E Omnibus, 1912'. (Photographer: Royal Engineers Official Photographer. Reproduced courtesy of the Imperial War Museum)

List of Maps

Introduction: The Shape of Britain

What is the shape of Britain? The British mainland measures just under 600 miles from top to toe. It is almost 300 miles across at its widest point. Its coastline is 11,000 miles long. Around it huddles a brood of more than 5,000 islands. And its distinctive silhouette, looking a little like a bob-tailed dog or a wingless dragon, is instantly recognisable on any map or globe. But jostling within that familiar profile are countless vying maps of the country. Some of these are founded on rock – or on the natural features of the land. But far more are built on dreams – on human activity, effort, and aspiration. This book is an exploration of just a few of them.

It is not a book about physical maps – either those that make mad bids for freedom on windy hilltops, or those that exist on microchips in our cars and phones. Real maps were indispensable in writing this book, but their history and uses, and the politics and aesthetics involved in that, are a vast subject which has been written about elsewhere. This book is more about people and the wonderful maps that exist in their minds. On one level, of course, there is a different map of Britain for every person who has ever lived in the country (or even visited it). Those maps, if they were ever drawn, would each be representations of lives lived – with beloved homes at their centres, elongated stretches of land where travel had been slow or difficult, and vast empty spaces where imagination faltered or trips ended. But there are also communities who share imaginative maps of the country. Maps of things that have been forgotten. Maps of things that are hidden. Maps of things that most of us have never even dreamt of. And those maps often lie at the heart of group identities and loyalties.

Writing each of this book's chapters was rather like discovering a series of new countries, hidden within Britain's borders. Some of these unfamiliar lands were surprisingly more spacious than the Britain we know from road atlases and OS maps. The pilot's Britain, with its vertical dimensions extending higher than Everest, has the capacity to accommodate thousands and still seem empty. The caver's Britain contains regions still waiting to be discovered, more unknown than the deepest jungle. And the canal map of Britain reveals a land that takes four or five days to cross. So viewed through the right lenses, I discovered, Britain is a surprisingly large small island.

It is also a country with countless competing centres. Of course, even those centres we are most familiar with are contested and subjective. If Britain's population was asked to locate its capital on an empty silhouette of the country, most would stick a pin somewhere along the serpentine course of the Thames. But some would instead tuck it neatly under the dragon's chin on the southern shore of the Firth of Forth, or just under Britain's bob-tail on the north coast of the Bristol Channel. Many would ask for two, three, or four pins. As a Yorkshire lass, mine might go in York, the old capital of the Danelaw.

Move away from politics and economics to passions and endeavours though, and the location of Britain's capital becomes even more uncertain. For meteorologists, the heart of Britain might be either Dalness in the Scottish Highlands (with the highest levels of annual rainfall), the Cairngorm mountains (the windiest spot in the country), or the Scilly Isles (the warmest place in Britain). The British surfing capital is generally agreed to be Newquay in Cornwall, with its annual competitions and festival – though other Cornish beaches also now claim that title.[1] And among climbers, the Peak District is usually hailed as Britain's climbing capital – its rock faces (empty to casual visitors) etched with more than 10,000 published routes on climbers' maps of the region.

The immovable grit-stone of the Peak District means that it will always be an important site on the climber's map of Britain. Other centres, though, are forever shifting. The capital of the lepidopter-ist's Britain is altogether more transient. At the last count, the richest area for butterfly spotting was a rough triangle of land mid-way along Britain's south coast, made up of the adjoining counties of Hampshire, Wiltshire and Dorset. But hot springtimes, wet summers, and changes in farming could easily move that fragile heart.[2] Or (to take an entirely different example) in 1861, Britain's crime capital was Gloucester, closely followed by Worcester: today it is Stratford in East London.

Shared knowledge of such national maps is in some cases a relatively recent phenomenon – before then, understanding was far more localised. It was only in 1976 that the first bird-watchers' map of Britain was created: *The Atlas of Breeding Birds in Britain and Ireland*, produced by the British Trust for Ornithology and the Irish Wildbird Conservancy, and based on the records of nearly 15,000 observers, which revealed the distribution of each species and there-fore the main centres for bird-watching in this country.[3] It was modelled on the Botanical Society of the British Isles' *Atlas of the British Flora*, which itself had only been published in 1962. The bird watching capital of Britain is now generally agreed to lie along the Norfolk coast – though the distribution of each species shifts suffi-ciently for the atlas to need redrawing every couple of decades, most recently as a four-year project that lasted from 2007 until 2011 and cost well over a million pounds.[4]

Sociological mapping of Britain began rather earlier. One of the earliest studies was Henry Mayhew's *London Labour and the London Poor: A Cyclopaedia of the Condition and Earnings of Those That Will Work, Those That Cannot Work, and Those That Will Not Work*, published first as a series of newspaper articles and then in 1861 as a book – from which survey comes Gloucester's dubious fame at that time. The study contained a selection of maps covered in ominous-looking black patches to reveal those areas of the country where illiteracy, pick-pocketing, or prostitution most flourished. On its overall map of Britain's criminal activity, a dark t-like shape stretches down the west of England from Lancaster to Somerset, with a curling tail reaching into Hampshire and an arm extending through Oxford and Middlesex as far as Essex.[5]

Mayhew's maps were broad-brushed. The inhabitants of quiet Hampshire villages at the time would no doubt have been horrified to see that they lived within a criminal hotspot simply by virtue of being in the same county as Portsmouth and Southampton. Today, the mapping of criminal activity in Britain is rather more precise. In fact, since the Home Office launched a crime-cataloguing website in 2011, it is now possible to pinpoint criminal centres down to individual roads or postcodes.[6] Other maps today are also very precise. Bird and butterfly populations are now mapped onto a grid spread across Britain like a vast butterfly net, with each square section just ten kilometres across.

Burglaries, birds, butterflies – conceptual maps of Britain have not only become more precise, they have also gradually become more specialised. Three centuries before Mayhew outlined the criminal shape of the country, topographical writers were the first people to begin the mapping of Britain in terms of historical, natural, and social interests. Their guidebooks were encyclopaedic in range. They contained the first published accounts of many of Britain's caves, stone circles, ancient churches, and curious folklore, and so constitute the earliest ancestors of many of the maps in this book. However, those records were part of a wonderful potpourri that also included descriptions of the hills, rivers, wildlife, bogs, and wealthiest families in each area.

Some of the sixteenth century's topographical works focused on one particular region, but the best-known and most influential of them was William Camden's 1586 *Britannia* whose ambitious scope stretched across the whole country. *Britannia* (after which this book is titled) has been credited as having instigated the 'rediscovery of England' that took place during the late sixteenth and early seventeenth century – the national realisation of how rich and diverse our country is.[7] One of the things that is most interesting about it, though, is that it is not just about England – it was one of the first tours of Britain to also look at sites of interest in Scotland, Ireland and Wales. This was twenty years before the union of Scotland's and England's crowns under James I and VI. So it was very much a book that cut across political borders. Certainly, it was hugely successful – initially published in Latin, it was soon reprinted in English, and was still being used as a standard reference work well into the nineteenth century, when both Scotland and Ireland had been politically united with England.

Like *Britannia*, this book aims to cut through the political borders that we are sometimes prone to mistake as natural and timeless divisions of our country. The invisible frontiers on the aeronautical map of Britain are a reminder that our national, county, and parish boundaries are for most of their courses equally intangible. While a few follow obvious natural features like the Rivers Wye or Tamar, others (like the Scottish–English border, which lies obstinately north of the River Tweed) are marked only intermittently by signs on major roads and by lonely waymarkers like the Three Counties Stone that marks the intersection of Cumbria, Yorkshire and Lancashire. These tokens are strung together like beads – by the strings of black dots and dashes on Ordnance Survey maps, but primarily by threads of imagination.

The caver's map of Britain is an illustration of the fact that rock (much like water) does not respect national or even county boundaries – as is the geologist's map, on which the Lake District mountain Helvellyn, for instance, is occasionally viewed as part of Scotland – on the grounds that in the distant prehistoric past, it broke off from the West Highlands, floated down the west coast of Britain, and eventually crashed into Cumbria.[8]

And the megalith hunter's map is a reminder that as soon as we begin looking back across time, Britain's modern boundaries begin to blur like a time-lapse photograph of cobwebs being spun and respun. Our county borders, of course, have been redrawn within many people's living memory. The Local Government Acts of 1972 and 1973, which turned Monmouthshire into Gwent and Ayr into Strathclyde, caused much anger and heartache at the time and even today, more than forty years later, many still cling to the memory of the old (now referred to as 'ceremonial') county borders. The Yorkshire Ridings Society is still fighting for 'a Yorkshire address for all parts of Yorkshire', while the Oxfordshire Association is involved in a long-term campaign for the erection of 'county stones' along the extremities of their historic county.

Gaze across the panorama of early history and prehistory, though, and the redrawing of sixteenth-century boundaries in 1972, although distressing to so many, begins to disappear in a constant shifting and shuffling of districts. For megalith hunters, the country has three meaningful districts, each characterised by a different building style, which splice the country diagonally. But ask an archaeologist where Britain's most important boundaries lie and they will probably give you a different answer for every few hundred years of prehistory. The earliest answer will be that around 600 BC, Britain was divided into five shadowy regions, each distinguished by regional fashions in crockery, ornaments, weapons, and buildings (the prehistoric equivalents of back-to-back terraces, oast houses, and flat caps) that cut across almost all of our current national borders.[9]

Borders are important to British identities. Indeed, they often take on an imaginative life of their own. The Watford Gap went from being a convenient low-lying pass that allowed easy travel between Birmingham and London, to being a theoretical boundary between different English dialects, to becoming a byword for the seemingly insurmountable economic and cultural differences between northern and southern England. Hadrian's Wall probably began life as a super-sized estate boundary – there more for ostentation than any practical function.[10] But in the centuries since its original meaning was forgotten, it has come to be viewed as the point at which invading Romans were firmly beaten back by the Scots (who resisted where the feeble English succumbed), and therefore as a symbolic barrier between England and Scotland (though it lies entirely in England).[11]

Admittedly, Britain's borders are necessary on many practical levels – to ensure that rubbish is collected and aeroplanes are separated. But the chapters here are a reminder that there are also other ways of defining communities, and other ways of imagining our relationship with the land that we live in. They should also remind us that maps of Britain are forever shifting and changing – gaps are constantly filled in on the pilots', cavers', and ley hunters' maps of the country. Busy thoroughfares disappear and then reappear on the canal map of Britain. Such mutability might make us wonder how the shape of Britain will be perceived in our grandchildren's lifetimes, or in their grandchildren's lives.

It may be that the country will be organised entirely differently from how many people think of it today. What now lies hidden and dragonish beneath Britain's surface could entirely alter the character of the country's surface, transforming rural areas into industrial heartlands, if the 'fracking' of natural gas reserves becomes commonplace. Or our quiet uplands – Dartmoor, the Yorkshire Dales, the Highlands – could become bustling residential areas if rising tides make coastal plains uninhabitable (and if so, this would be a curious reversal of the depopulation that many of these areas have seen since prehistoric times).

Our current political borders could be replaced by, say, an east–west boundary, following the Pennines down the spine of Britain. It is an idea that is not quite as silly as it sounds, since Britain's prevailing weather patterns all travel from west to east. Estate agents and economists are increasingly thinking about the country in those terms.[12] And many archaeologists, looking at Britain over millennia, consider that it makes far more sense to think about the country culturally in terms of an East–West divide than in terms of the North–South rift that is written about so much in the popular press.[13]

But even if Britain's official shape were to change on OS maps, sat-navs, and world atlases, for many communities those new divisions would have little bearing on what was most important in their everyday lives – on their values, their affiliations, and their sense of identity. Just as any chart of the night sky represents only a fraction of what really exists up there in the illimitable space beyond our planet, so too any published map of Britain will always be merely an outline of what is most obvious – what can be picked out with least difficulty. Beyond that, there will always be number-less constellations of ideas: vague glimmerings which, once the eye is trained upon them, sharpen into intriguing universes within the familiar lines of the horizon we once thought we knew.

Major
Caving Sit[es]
of Britain

ORKNEY

LEWIS

Allt Nan Uamh
Stream Cave
Cnoc Nan Uamh
Uamh An Claonite

SCOTLAND

CUMBRIA

Bullpot Farm
Casterton Fell
Lancaster Hole
Ease Gill
Caverns
Pippikin Pot
Casterton
Gavel
Bye George
Yordas
Cave
Jingle
(Gingle)
Pot
Lost John's Cave
Weathercote
Cave
Leck
Fell
Notts Pot
Leck
Ireby Fell Cavern
Ireby
Fell
Large Pot
Hurtle
Pot
Rift
Pot
Low Douk
Cave
YORKSHIRE
LANCS
Ireby
Kingsdale
Master Cave
White Scar Cave
Al[e]
P[…]
Ingleton
Gaping Gill

Yordas Cave
The Three Counties System
Manchester Hole
White Scar Cave
Gaping Gill

Titan
Peak Cavern
Ogof Hesp Alyn
Poole's
Cavern
Cresswell Crags Caves
Eldon Hole
Ogof Llyn Du
Ogof Dydd Brafon
ENGLAND

WALES

Miss Grace's
Lane Swallet
Dan Yr Ogof
Ogof-yr-Esgyrn
Slaughter Stream Cave
Ogof Ffynnon Ddu
Ogof
Draenen
Clearwell Caves
Cat Hole
Penpark Hole
Charterhouse Cave
Upper Flood Swallet
Swildon's Hole
St Cuthbert's Swallet
Wookey Hole

Chudleigh
Cavern
Pridhamsleigh Cavern
Kent's Cavern
Baker's Pit

| 0 | 20 | 40 | 60 | 80 | 100 |
| 0 | 25 | 50 | 75 | 100 | 125 | 150 kilo[…] |

I

Underground, Overground: The Caver's Map of Britain

Until the middle of the nineteenth century, the hills and mountains of Great Britain had an unsettling tendency to move. Not Jehovah-style, but still, their heights and relative places in the national records shifted irritatingly around from decade to decade and from century to century. In the second half of the eighteenth century, the flat-topped hulk of Ingleborough – one of Yorkshire's three peaks – varied between 3,987 and 5,280 feet on maps of the county (its actual height is just 2,372 feet).[1] And until the early 1800s, Cosdon Beacon – the rounded Dartmoor hill that watches paternally over the villages of South Zeal, Sticklepath and Belstone – was adjudged the highest point in south-west England. It was not until the Principal Triangulation of Great Britain had ventured into the interior of Dartmoor, and the first Ordnance Survey map of the moor had been produced in 1809, that it quickly became apparent that the title had been inaccurately bestowed – owing to the illusion of height created by the lowlands to the north of the hill – and Cosdon was swiftly deposed by the small rocky summit of Yes Tor.[2]

In these days of satellite mapping, mountains in Britain tend to stay where you put them. Pianos can reliably be hauled up Ben Nevis without discovering, on return to base, that the blasted rock down the valley is an inch or two taller. Yet venture beneath Britain's crust and the map of the country becomes almost as mutable as those seventeenth-century charts with whole islands missing. The caver's map of Britain is being so constantly redrawn that by the time this book is in print, South Wales may have become bigger than Yorkshire, and Derbyshire may have grown deeper.

Chris Jewell of the British Caving Association (which maintains the National Cave Registry) explains to me that just as the surface-dweller might bag the highest Munros, walk the country's longest valleys or climb its tallest cliff faces, so Britain's underground landscape possesses a variety of natural highlights (or perhaps 'lowlights'), sites of pilgrimage that feature on every caver's map of the country. A cave might be famed as the deepest from ceiling to base, feared as the most intricate of mazes, or renowned as the longest system of passages underground. A pothole (distinguished from a cave by its vertical rather than horizontal form) might have the longest drop in Britain, or else the largest chamber.

On a blazing August bank holiday weekend, I visit one of those caving shrines. Gaping Gill in Yorkshire lies on the southern slopes of Ingleborough. The largest underground chamber to open naturally to the surface, this abyss of dizzying proportions is 140 metres long, 27 metres wide and 34 metres deep. York Minster would fit snugly inside. The chasm also contains the tallest unbroken waterfall in Britain, where Fell Beck tumbles suicidally from its happy course between low tufted banks into the yawning depths below. Its crashing fall to the bottom is twice the height of Niagara. Today, a small village of brightly coloured tents perches around the entrance to the pothole. Every August bank holiday since 1932, this hole in the ground has been a magnet not just for cavers but for curious members of the public like myself, who are winched one by one to the bottom by members of Craven Pothole Club.

The descent to the base, enclosed in an outsized canary cage, takes just minutes. Once on the boulder-strewn floor, I gaze in bewilderment at the circle of bright sky far above and the treacherous overhanging ledges between myself and the way out. If that winch were to break down . . . What fascinates me more than the huge, chilly cavern itself, though, is a small group of cavers, helmeted and wellied, carrying ropes and other gear. For them the gill is not the pinnacle of the day's adventure, but merely the starting point from which to explore the 17-kilometre maze of passages that extends between here and Clapham. One by one they post themselves into a narrow horizontal slot at the top of a large slope of boulders, and disappear. The Alice part of me feels an irresponsible urge to follow, but the dimensions of this doorway are appalling. I am left with the sensation of teetering on a threshold between this Britain and a wonderland beyond.

The festive atmosphere of the bank holiday winch trips is a far cry from the first successful descent of Gaping Gill in August 1895. Much to the irritation of locals, who had made repeated attempts to conquer the pothole since 1842 and had been planning a fresh assault since 1893, this feat was accomplished by a Frenchman, Edouard Alfred Martel, an experienced potholer and prolific author on the caves of his homeland.[3] It took Martel 23 minutes, climbing down rope ladders in the icy spray of Fell Beck, to reach the base of Gaping Gill, and another 28 minutes of being hauled up on a lifeline to get out. Looking up from the base of the chasm, however, he recorded that the view past the waterfall to the sky beyond was 'one of the most extraordinary spectacles it has ever been my pleasure to witness'.[4] Martel made incredibly accurate sketches of Gaping Gill and observed that the chamber 'could contain a cathedral with the spire running up the shaft'.[5] In May 1896, he was emulated by local potholer Edward Calvert, who on this his second attempt on Gaping Gill became not only the first Englishman to set foot on the floor of the pothole, but also the first person to properly survey it, revealing its full extent. For a full century after Calvert took his triangulation equipment into Gaping Gill, the pothole was revered among cavers as the largest in the country.

All that changed on 1 January 1999. Just as Ingleborough, in the late eighteenth century, lost its crown as highest mountain in England, so two centuries later, Gaping Gill was relegated on the map of subterranean Britain. On that New Year's Day, Dave Nixon, now one of Britain's premier cave explorers, scrambled into an unknown chamber beneath Derbyshire's Peak District. In the darkness it was initially impossible to tell whether the chasm was ten feet high or a hundred. In fact, after Nixon had spent six days climbing to its top, he came to the astonishing realisation that the chamber – Titan, as he fittingly named it – was 464 feet high, or 141.5 metres, equal in height to the London Eye. This vast abyss had lain unsuspected, and yet only a short distance below ground. 'It's amazing to think people on the surface would have had no idea that it was there,' Nixon reminisces. 'If you stand in the right place, there's ten metres of moor under your feet, then 145 metres of open space.'[6]

The discovery of Titan is not the only dramatic transformation of the map of underground Britain to have occurred in recent years. On 6 November 2011, below that western corner of the Dales where the counties of Yorkshire, Lancashire and Cumbria jostle each other like irritable bedfellows, two meandering underground labyrinths were reconnected for the first time in millennia. Together they formed what became known as the Three Counties system – a vast subterranean metropolis, which with more than 90 kilometres of passages extending across a trio of counties is now indisputably the Greater London of Britain's underworld.

Like any British city, this hidden capital is made up of distinct districts and neighbourhoods, each with its own character. Ease Gill Caverns to the north has broad 'trunk passages' running through it like underground A roads, and is home to five species of bat. Pippikin, just south of that, is a mature cave system – the 'old town' of the underground capital – formed by streams that have long since migrated elsewhere, leaving behind strikingly decorated passageways. Lost Johns' is a newer and mostly flooded area, while to the far south of the system, Large Pot is perhaps the Canary Wharf of this subterranean city, with the most extensive and complex vertical geography.[7] 'It's got an awful lot of variety,' says Andy Walsh, who was part of the team that connected up the Three Counties system. 'Whenever you find new sections, they're completely different to other bits.'[8]

What is also truly remarkable is that from the grey-green sheep-dotted hillsides around Casterton you would scarcely guess that you were standing directly above such a subterranean conurbation. A few of the Three Counties' 'city gates', such as the entrance to Lost Johns', are obvious enough – there a large stream tumbles dramatically underground. Consequently it was explored to a limited extent early in the cave system's human history – certainly in 1928, but perhaps far earlier according to an 1888 account, which claims that the cave was named for two lost explorers.[9] The hole into which those unlucky candle-bearing cavers may have descended, however, is just one of at least 44 known entrances to the Three Counties system, the majority of which are as well concealed as foxholes, hidden beneath heather or between rocks.

The serious exploration and piecing together of the Three Counties cave system began from one such innocuous-looking recess. The story goes that on 29 September 1946, two Lancaster men, George Cornes and Bill Taylor, were sitting on Casterton Fell in Cumbria when they noticed that the grass close by them was quivering in a breeze. They traced the draught to a small, overgrown gravelly hollow.[10] Today this unassuming entrance, now known as Lancaster Hole, which alarmingly opens immediately on to a 110-foot-deep shaft, remains one of the most popular (if terrifying) ways into the Ease Gill part of the Three Counties system. In the weeks and months after Cornes and Taylor's discovery, members of the British Speleological Association explored the network of passages radiating out from Lancaster Hole.[11] What they gradually revealed was a long, dry ancient stream bed with clusters of passages branching off it like the fronds of some gigantic fossilised fern. By 1968, the known cave system was 12 miles long. Two years later, a neighbouring cave, Pippikin Pot – previously believed impassable – was explored, and by the end of the 1970s that had been connected to the Ease Gill caverns, adding its five miles of passages to the total length of the system and extending Ease Gill across one county border, from Cumbria into Lancashire.

Over subsequent years, further caves were discovered and connected to Ease Gill, like villages being swallowed into the suburbs of some inexorably mushrooming subterranean city. The next dramatic enlargement came in 1989, when divers discovered long flooded passages that expanded the cave system well into Lancashire, connecting it with Lost Johns' cave. And by the start of the twenty-first century, claims for the overall length of the Ease Gill caves varied across different published guides from around 70 to 100 kilometres as competing surveyors – like overly optimistic city planners – incorporated both actual and projected 'suburbs' into its official size. Ease Gill's pre-eminence as the longest cave system in Britain was not to remain unchallenged, however. In August 2010, a new and detailed survey conceded that at that time it was actually just 60 kilometres long. Although still substantial, this meant that it not only lost between a seventh and two-fifths of its proclaimed length in one fell swoop; it was also instantly deprived of its place as the capital of Britain's underland.[12]

Its place was taken by Ogof Draenen, South Wales's 'Hawthorne Cave'. For many years this cavern had been considered as short and inconsequential as its namesake tree, neither penetrating much deeper than the subsoil of a hillside above Abergavenny. On 6 October 1994, however, members of the Morgannwg Caving Club had cleared a way through a mess of collapsed boulders inside the known cave to reveal unsuspected passages beyond. Newly discovered caves, like unknown seams of oil or gold, are often closely guarded secrets in the caving world. However, Ogof Draenen's discoverers took the unusual step of inviting other cavers to find whatever caves they could. The result of this collaborative effort was that within just one month, more than 20 kilometres of new passages had been identified – a record for British caving. By 1997, Draenen was 70 kilometres long, making it in fact the longest cave in Britain, although like many an eighteenth-century mountain, its status was not recognised until more than a decade later.

One of the first cavers invited to help unearth and map Ogof Draenen's secret passages was Tarquin Wilton-Jones, now the compiler of the UK Caves Database. Cavers had long predicted the existence of a large cave somewhere in the vicinity of Draenen, he explains to me, simply because of the way in which streams mysteriously sink and rise in the hillsides. What they found, however, 'almost immediately surpassed expectations'.[13] The typical passage size in Ogof Draenen, Wilton-Jones tells me, 'is about ten by ten metres in cross section – that's wide enough to hold three lanes of traffic. The largest passages are just under 20 metres square – enough to hold an entire motorway, with four double-decker buses stacked on top of each other. And the largest chambers are about 50 to 100 metres across, and 30 metres high – roughly the area of a football pitch, and taller than Buckingham Palace.'[14]

While these dimensions mean that stooping is seldom necessary, Draenen is nevertheless one of underground Britain's most challenging environments. Its sheer size means that trips into its interior need to be lengthier than many seasoned cavers are accustomed to – Wilton-Jones himself has often spent stints of almost three days' duration inside. It is also an old cave, abandoned millennia ago by the waters that once formed it, and like a grand but neglected colonial city is now prone to collapsing ceilings and crumbling decoration. It has 'spectacular stal formations – grand stalagmites, intricate helictites and aragonite needles, gypsum crystals and crystal pools. And some of the most amazing collections of fossils in their natural setting,' Wilton-Jones enthuses. However, he concedes, 'It's hard to admire them when you're slipping and stumbling over kilometres of boulders. You spend more time looking at your feet than the cave.'

For this reason, Draenen is not generally one of Britain's best-loved caves. But those cavers who know it well – especially those who were involved in its discovery – are devoted admirers of the system. For Wilton-Jones it was a serious injustice that for over a decade it was incorrectly listed as shorter than Ease Gill and was 'denied its rightful recognition' as the longest cave system in Britain. 'It's a cave that I have a very soft spot for,' he confesses, 'so I would have liked it to have got the recognition that it deserved.'[15]

Sadly for Tarquin Wilton-Jones, and the other discoverers of Ogof Draenen, their cave was not given long to enjoy its pre-eminence on the map of subterranean Britain. Even as celebrations were under way in Wales, deep beneath Lancashire work was going on to dramatically extend the Ease Gill system. As early as 1968, when those caves were just twelve miles long, there had been speculation that they could form part of 'a single cave complex on an enormous scale', straddling Cumbria, Lancashire and Yorkshire.[16] It was that dream that fuelled the gradual expansion of Ease Gill over subsequent decades, and its realisation came closer in May 2010, when caves in North Yorkshire were connected to Ireby Fell Cavern in Lancashire. That left just one missing link – between Notts Pot and Lost Johns' caves – in order to join the Yorkshire–Lancashire cave system with the Cumbria–Lancashire one to create a vast complex straddling the three counties.

Although the way to connect those systems was first confidently identified in 2009, 140 metres of collapsed rock stood obstreperously in the way of the Three Counties vision. The mission of clearing it was taken up by a group of almost fifty cavers, led by Tim Allen, Andy Walsh, and Hugh St Lawrence. Calling themselves the 'Misty Mountain Mud Miners', this subterranean brotherhood laboured with dwarfish persistence for more than two years, gathering every week deep beneath Leck Fell to smash fallen rocks, cart oozing sediment up to the surface, patiently buttress their newly cleared passages with scaffolding, and pump out flooded areas. 'It was,' Andy Walsh says, 'a bit like the First World War. We thought it'd be done by Christmas. But it really turned into a war of attrition. It was like the worst kind of nightmare.'[17]

Hopes of a breakthrough came slowly. By January 2010, a whispering breeze was insinuating its way into Lyle Caverns from Notts Pot. By August of that year, sounds could be faintly heard between the two cave systems.[18] But it was not until 6 November 2011 that light could be glimpsed through a tiny hole in the rock. 'First we heard voices, then we saw a light,' Hugh St Lawrence remembers. 'After a few hours we managed to pass a crowbar through the small hole, and soon after that we shook hands with the team on the other side. Eventually we could pass through. It was a fantastic moment.'[19]

Most of the cavers who worked on the Three Counties connection lived locally – around the Lancashire villages of Heysham and Grange, Cumbria's Kendal, or Yorkshire's Ingleton. While Britain's subterranean explorers may travel the length and breadth of the country to undertake underground quests, many cherish a particular affection for the caves of their home area. Tarquin Wilton-Jones, who lives 'virtually on top of Ogof Draenen', has, by his own admission, 'a love affair with it'.[20] This is partly because, like their overground counterparts, each major subterranean province of Britain has its own distinctive character. Take Dave Nixon blindfolded into a cave and he could tell you whether or not he was in Derbyshire. 'The caves in the Dales are cleaner than the Peak District caves. They're well washed. Derbyshire caves are smaller and muddier,' he explains. 'There are also different mineral deposits. There are mineral deposits that we have here that are extremely rare. Particularly the Blue John – a blue-stained calcium fluorite.'[21]

The Peak District is also distinctive for the number of natural caves that combine with and are often accessed via lead mines, some of them dating back as far as Roman times. It is perhaps to underground Britain what Cornwall is to its surface – on the one hand an area still marked with the signs of an intensive industrial history; on the other, a Mecca for tourists. The area around Castleton has a total of four show caves and a long history as a destination for pleasure-seekers and the curious. In 1129, Peak

Cavern was hailed as the 'First Wonder of Britain' by Henry, Archbishop of Huntingdon, in his *Historia Anglorum*. From 1622, the 'Seven Wonders of the Peak' (which included more than one cave) were promoted to tourists after Michael Drayton published his series of poems by that title. And in 1880, Queen Victoria attended a concert within the dark recesses of Peak Cavern.

Much of the distinctive character of underground British regions, like the country's surface, is a result of geology. Because of the angle of the limestone bed in both Derbyshire and the Dales, cave systems there tend to be very vertical, with lots of potholes, whereas the caves in Mendip are fairly shallow and those in South Wales even more horizontal. 'A classic underground trip in the Dales would start at an open hole and head steeply down,' explains Chris Jewell.[22] These entrances might be huge yawning chasms (like Gaping Gill), secret slits on remote fellsides searched out using grid references, or unimpressive-looking holes that the casual passer-by would dismiss as a drain or an animal den. Starting Handle Hole, for example, looks like nothing more exciting than a manhole hidden on a roadside verge next to Leck Fell car park (its name taken from a car starting handle found inside). Most of the caves, however, are wet. 'In Yorkshire, you're usually following an underground stream all the way,' Jewell continues, 'going down lots of steep shafts and using ropes until it finally levels out.'[23] Such Dales trips typically end at a sump – a section of completely flooded passage.

Besides Gaping Gill and the Ease Gill system, other attractions on the caver's map of Yorkshire include Alum Pot, with its 140-foot sheer drop of an entrance, and Manchester Hole, once believed to be a subterranean route to the city after which it is named, and now a popular destination for school groups. Such sites can be nearly as busy below ground as the overland attractions of the Dales. Even on a weekend in December, cavers might arrive at a popular Dales pothole only to find that, like the car park at the Brontë village of Haworth, it is full for the day.[24] This has been the case since the early twentieth century, when many of today's caving clubs were formed. At Whitsuntide 1929, members of Yorkshire's Gritstone Club 'regarded with some dismay' the queues of potholers waiting to descend into the Lost Johns' cave system.[25] Today cavers book their descent into the same deep recess at least three months in advance.[26]

One virtue of the Dales area, however, is that, despite its popularity among cavers, with 285 kilometres of known passages (the distance from Leeds to Bristol), it is still relatively easy to find a pot of one's own to descend into, away from the most celebrated grottos. Indeed, the region contains as many caves as all the other parts of Britain put together. Those disappointed young Gritstoners in 1929 ambled off to poke into a couple of unnamed holes and chanced upon Pippikin Pot, which now forms part of the Ease Gill System. Those halcyon days of casual discovery have long gone. 'All the easy projects were done in the fifties,' Dave Nixon laments. 'You don't just walk into a new cave these days in Britain.'[27] Nonetheless, riddled as it is like a Swiss cheese, the Dales area still proffers the promise of new caves to discover. 'Unless you're really lucky, it's difficult to find new caves in the Peak District or Mendip,' according to Nixon (who was, of course, unbelievably lucky himself), 'but in the Yorkshire Dales or in South Wales you might easily find a new few hundred metres.'

After the Dales, South Wales is probably the second dark heart of underground Britain. Besides Ogof Draenen, many other caves there are also vast – including Ogof Ffynnon Ddu (or the Cave of the Black Spring), which is currently the deepest cave in Britain at 308 metres, or 1,010 feet. In total, South Wales has over 250 kilometres, or 155 miles, of caves. Like Draenen, the majority of these contain huge passages, formed long ago. 'In many caving areas of England,' Tarquin Wilton-Jones explains, 'the caves are local drainage systems – relatively recent developments that provide underground routes for local streams. They tend to have smaller passages, and are usually clean-washed, with significant vertical sections.' By contrast, subterranean South Wales has 'horizontal caves that once served as the drainage routes for meltwater at the edge of the ice sheet, near the end of the last ice age. They carried vast amounts of water through large conduits, traversing entire mountains.'

These ancient riverways, now abandoned by the waters that formed them and encrusted with fossils, are like the giant galleries of a subterranean natural history museum. In them one sees 'a cross section through the ages of the life that populated the area over 300 million years before – the shells, the coral, the bones of the sharks that swam in a carboniferous ocean, the remains of animals hunted by prehistoric peoples'.[28] For Wilton-Jones, the antiquity and sheer size of the subterranean region beneath South Wales makes it the Scottish Highlands of underground Britain: 'It's not to everyone's taste. But it's remote, wild and challenging, with some incredible views and rewards [. . .] somewhere where you can challenge your endurance, experience isolation, and feel what it's really like to be ten hours of hard exercise from the nearest phone reception.'

The time and effort needed to journey through the South Wales underground is not just due to the cave systems' sheer size. Many of the larger systems, like Draenen, are also known for the complexity of their geography, with labyrinthine passages that weave a long and tortuous path beneath ground – sometimes with as much as 15 kilometres of cave passage beneath just one kilometre of the surface. Here is the spaghetti junction of underground Britain, with numerous complicated intersections.

I wonder how one navigates around underground Britain – what landmarks do cavers use? Tarquin Wilton-Jones might find his way, he says, by reference to 'the shape of a flake of rock, or the colour of a certain stalactite'. Other cavers might build a cairn at a junction as a reminder – much like those on the Lake District's felltops. Occasionally they might even resort, Theseus style, to using string. 'Imagine walking at night with a bright torch, following a series of streams,' Wilton-Jones explains. 'Now turn around and try to recognise each stream junction to get yourself back to the start.' Chris Jewell describes the experience similarly. It is, he says, very much a memory game – a question of remembering particular passageways and striking rock formations. Of course, numerous guides are published for established and popular cave systems – the OS maps of subterranean Britain – but many cavers prefer not to carry these below ground, and in any case they tend to read in one direction only and reversing them is often difficult. 'What's key,' Jewell says, 'is always looking behind you on the way in.'

The region beneath the Mendip Hills and the Avon valley in the south-west of England is one of the easiest British areas to navigate below ground. After the Dales, Derbyshire and South Wales (in no particular order), this is the next most important site on the caver's map of Britain. Few of its caves exceed 500 feet in depth, or a mile or two in length, so finding your way around is relatively straight-forward. Partly for this reason, it is also one of the busiest caving areas in Britain. In Swildon's Hole, south of Bristol, you are hardly more likely to find yourself alone than on the beach at Weston-super-Mare. Aficionados of the area, however, praise its variety, pointing out its 'noisy streamways, fine grottos, squeezes, and large chambers often all in the same cave'.[29]

The Mendips area is also well known as a cave-diving hotspot, attracting divers in the same way that surfers flock to the south-west's beaches every summer. The deepest sump discovered so far in Britain – a shivering 90 metres of dark, unlit water – lies in Wookey Hole. And far beneath the Mendip Hills is the largest underground river system in Britain – the 54-square-kilometre catchment area for the Cheddar Yeo river. Dye tests have shown that some of the water in this subterranean morass travels beneath ground for up to ten miles, taking fourteen days to reach the town of Cheddar.[30]

Unsurprisingly, it was the watery recesses of this region that attracted the very first attempts at cave-diving in Britain. In 1934, a team of caving enthusiasts led by Graham Balcombe successfully sent one of its members, Jack Shepherd, through 300 metres of unknown, flooded passages in Swildon's Hole, armed with a home-made rubber suit and breathing apparatus fed by a bicycle pump.[31] A year later, the same team turned their attention to Wookey Hole, this time equipped with borrowed Royal Navy diving equipment. On 14 July, Balcombe took his first tentative steps below water (the equipment being so heavy that swimming was entirely out of the question). His log of the expedition recalls: 'The first trip up the bed of the River Axe is a revelation of the beauties of this underwater world. It is almost impossible to describe the feelings as leaving the surface [. . .] one suddenly enters an utterly different world, a world of green, where the waters are as clear as crystal.'[32]

During the course of that year, the divers gradually succeeded in penetrating further and further into the flooded sections of Wookey: from chamber three, the last dry section, to chamber seven, where they used floats and ladders in order to climb up to an air chamber never seen before by man. There their progress was halted, not simply because of the rudimentary nature of their equipment, but also because of a worm discovered in a kitchen sink in the village of Wookey; the unfortunate divers were imme-diately accused of muddying the local water supply.[33]

Unimaginable quantities of oozing, sucking mud is an impedi-ment to be contended with in many of Britain's cave systems. According to the University of Bristol's nonagenarian Speleological Society, subterranean Devon in particular is ideal for 'mud-wrestling midgets', being mostly distinguished by its 'small passages and copious amounts of mud'.[34] Devon has sufficient caves to be classed as an outlying minor province on the caver's map of Britain – as does the Forest of Dean, North Wales, and Assynt, in the Highlands of Scotland.

What Devon does possess, however, besides its mud, is one of Britain's most visited show caves. Kent's Cavern in Torquay, if we are to believe an inscription found within it – 'William Petre 1571' – has been attracting curious visitors for over four hundred years.

Today it draws around 80,000 tourists a year – as many as Wales's Caerphilly Castle or Scotland's Burns Museum. On the caver's map of the country, of course, Kent's Cavern is to the Ease Gill System or Ogof Draenen rather like what Richmond Park is to the Scottish Highlands: a tamed, pocket-sized and cheerily populous taster of Britain's subterranean world: a nice place to take the kids. Show caves in Britain were not always such safe environments, however. In the late eighteenth century, when the first ticket booths were installed by the mouths of notable caves, the guide leading visitors around Poole's Cavern in the Peak District used, in one section of the cavern, to 'desire you to lean towards the rock lest you should fall down a chasm', while the women selling candles outside were also responsible for allowing 'such a certain time [. . .] and if the visitors do not return when it is expired, they come in with fresh lights lest any accident should have happened'.[35]

Even now, there is not always a clear distinction between show caves and 'cavers' caves'. In Wales's Dan Yr Ogof, bedraggled parties of wetsuited cave explorers occasionally brush shoulders with jeans-and-trainer-clad tourists as they re-emerge into an electrically illuminated world after long, dark expeditions through the subterranean miles of passage that lie beyond the end of the show cave. Similarly, in both Somerset's Wookey Hole and Yorkshire's Ingleborough Cave, the same cave system contains both wide, family-friendly passages, and some of the most challenging cave dives in the country; it is simply a question of how far in one ventures.

In total, Britain has more than 30 show caves.[36] The biggest groupings are, unsurprisingly, in four of the principal caving centres – the Peak District, South Wales, south-west England, and Yorkshire (which boasts the longest show cave in the country, White Scar Cave). Several small show caves also exist in the south-east of England, in counties that barely register on the caver's map. In the main, however, these are man-made chasms, such as West Wycombe Caves in Buckinghamshire (the former residence of the notorious Hell Fire Club) and Chislehurst Caves in Kent – which are in fact both chalk mines. In 1903, William Nichols, then vice-president of the British Archaeological Association, speculated that Chislehurst Caves were Druidic, Roman and Saxon in origin. In fact, there is no evidence of them existing before around 1250. However, his theories excited a flurry of tourism to the site, and today the three main sections of the 'caves' still retain the names of their supposed excavators, while guides will point out ominous-looking subterranean Druidic altars – which are in fact benches for eighteenth-century miners.

The guides at Chislehurst also habitually point out a mammoth's tooth to visitors. This is actually no more than a piece of flint embedded in the chalk.[37] However, dotted across the subterranean map of Britain are several caves with a prehistoric heritage as rich and antique as any site above ground. Many of the visitors to Kent's Cavern, for instance, are drawn there not for the fine display of stalactites and stalagmites, but to view the best collection of cave bear remains to be found anywhere in Britain. The Torquay cave also boasts a human jawbone, dated at between 38,000 and 40,000 years old, making it one of the oldest fossils from modern man ever to have been found in Europe.

Only a few of Britain's 'bone caves' have been developed into public show caves. Rhinoceros, bear, mammoth and lion bones, left behind by both men and hyenas, are among the attractions that continue to draw visitors to Wookey Hole. Ogof-yr-Esgyrn (the Cave of the Bones) in Wales was discovered in the 1940s to house 42 Bronze Age human skeletons – and now forms the central attraction of the National Showcaves Centre near Swansea. And at the caves in Creswell Crags in Derbyshire, the discovery of thousands of animal bones – some of them carved 12,000 years ago into daggers, drinking vessels, needles and other tools – has (along with the cave's rock art) created a thriving visitor attraction with ambitions for a multimillion-pound expansion. Such sites are the Stonehenges of underground Britain, complete with their own car parks, interpretation panels, and fibreglass cavemen. Elsewhere, though, are subterranean necropolises that remain the province of Britain's cavers alone.

Close to Ullapool, in the north-west of Scotland, the bone caves of Inchnadamph have so far yielded up the bones of four humans, all well over 4,000 years old, as well as the remains of polar bears, reindeer, wolves and other creatures. This unique tableau of life in prehistoric Scotland has only emerged reluctantly, however: explorers have been retrieving remains from the subterranean national heritage site since the late nineteenth century, and the latest find – the almost complete skeleton of a large brown bear – was painstakingly recovered piecemeal by cave-divers from Grampian Speleological Group who braved Inchnadamph's tortuous flooded passages over a twelve-year period.

As bone caves demonstrate, subterranean Britain first began to be visited by humans – for shelter, sanctuary, storage, mining, or simply to marvel at, revere and adorn the rock – tens of thousands of years ago. A handful of caves continued to serve as hermitages, refuges or cells through the country's early recorded history.[38] However, the mapping of underground Britain did not begin until the seventeenth century, when the earliest survey of a British cave was published in the *Philosophical Transactions* of the Royal Society. The author of this work – Captain Samuel Sturmey, a retired mariner – descended in 1669 into Pen Park Hole, a pothole now squeezed between a housing estate and a golf course in the northern suburbs of Bristol. His detailed account was published thirteen years later, along with the survey of a Captain Collins, who had descended into the chasm in 1682; it was also included in Robert Atkins' 1779 *History of Gloucestershire*.[39]

Sturmey made his descent into Pen Park Hole by being lowered on ropes by a miner employed for the enterprise. Once down, he observed the horseshoe form of the chasm, and the rocks exposed inside. Spotting a cave leading off from the pothole, he was also intent on exploring this – or, rather, on sending the miner into the unknown void. 'I got a ladder down to us, and the Mine-Man went up the ladder to that place, and walked into it, about 70 paces, till he had just lost sight of me,' he recalled. This promising quest quickly ran out of steam, however, for the miner 'returned affrighted by the sight of an evil spirit, which we cannot persuade him but he saw, and for that reason will go thither no more'.[40] Sturmey was more successful in his other objective, however: his aim of proving that the water that rose and fell in the pothole was unconnected with that of the Severn estuary. 'I proved to the contrary,' he concluded, 'by staying there from three hours flood to two hours ebb, in which time we found no alteration in this river. Besides its waters are fresh, sweet and cool.'[41]

Sturmey has a good claim to stand at the very vanguard of all subsequent speleologists and cave explorers who have meticulously traced dye, smoke, or the dirt from a sheep wash through the course of subterranean streams and passages to contribute to the mapping of underground Britain. And he might well have made further discoveries about the form of Pen Park Hole – or at least his hired miner might have done so, once his nerve had returned. However, just four days after his descent into the pothole, Sturmey 'was troubled with an unusual and violent headache, which he imputed to his being in that vault, and falling from his head-ache into a fever, he soon after died'.[42]

Collins' 1682 survey of the pothole added little to Sturmey's account, except for more precise measurement. But Pen Park Hole features again in the history of subterranean Britain in 1775, as the site of the first recorded caving fatality. On 17 March of that year, the Reverend Thomas Newnam, one of the minor canons of Bristol Cathedral, visited Pen Park with another gentleman and two young ladies. Newnam was apparently curious about the precise depth of the pothole and decided to try measuring it by holding on to an overhanging ash tree and dropping a line into the void. The branch he was holding broke and he fell 'in the sight of the gentleman and the two young ladies, neither of whom could possibly afford him the least assistance'.[43]

An air of mystery enveloped Newnam's death owing to the total disappearance of his body in the pothole for several weeks before it bobbed back to the surface. This conundrum led to much speculation in the press and, thanks to the typically Victorian taste for the macabre, for several weeks it drew large crowds daily to the cave.[44] Several of these nineteenth-century ambulance-chasers were so intrigued that a system of ropes was set up to lower them into the pothole itself. One man who descended into the chasm was George Catcott – a pewterer by trade, but better known as the first patron of the Bristol forger Thomas Chatterton, as the brother of the anti-Newtonian clergyman and author Alexander Catcott, and as a local eccentric who had once climbed across the unfinished Bristol Bridge in order to claim the title of first man to pay the toll.

Catcott first descended into Pen Park Hole three days after the accident, and then again a month later. Seventeen years after this, his notes from the two visits were combined in *A Descriptive Account of a Descent Made into Pen-park Hole*, which was published in Bristol along with a copperplate engraving of the cavern. Although he stated in the preface to this work that it would make 'no attempts to explain and account for the causes or formation' of the cave, Catcott's patent motivation for surveying the pothole was to add grist to his brother Alexander's contention that the Old Testament deluge had been worldwide, and had been caused when waters trapped under the earth's crust broke free.[45] After carefully detailing the appearance and size of Pen Park Hole, George concluded that it 'could not have been made by art (as some have absurdly asserted) but by the retreat of the waters which flowed thro [. . .] into the great abyss beneath, at the time of the universal deluge'.

Catcott's geology may make us scoff today, but he did come up with a plausible answer to the mystery of Thomas Newnam's missing corpse, conjecturing that the body must have bobbed up into the air cavity above an adjoining cavern, only returning to the main chamber of Pen Park Hole once the water table had dropped.

Like Sturmey, then, he stands in the vanguard of those who first tried to trace and understand the shape of underground Britain. Catcott's minor contribution to this enterprise has of course only been remembered because he was in a position to publish his report. However, his narrative also provides fascinating glimpses of the (often rather more adventurous) exploration being undertaken by other amateurs in this period, as part of the emerging world of British caving. He records, for instance, that a land surveyor named Mr White had succeeded in linking Pen Park Hole with another pothole, 120 feet to the east, by having 'forced himself through upon his belly [. . .] with the utmost difficulty, and not without great hazard'.[46] And he concludes his account with a letter from Jeremiah Milles, dean of Exeter Cathedral, who had himself ventured into 'Wokey Hole, and caverns at the Peak and Pool's' (both Peak District caves).[47]

Catcott's account is the second earliest book to have been published about Britain's caves. The earliest is John Hutton's 1780 volume, *A Tour to the Caves in the Environs of Ingleborough and Settle*. This first appeared as an addendum to the second edition of Thomas West's *Guide to the Lakes* but was evidently popular enough to have been republished later the same year as a work in its own right, with a second edition following hot on its heels in 1781. Hutton had first written on the subject of Yorkshire's caves in 1761, in an article for *The Gentleman's Magazine*, and the book was an elaboration of this essay. It relates how the author, a Westmorland clergyman, made an unplanned diversion to visit the caves in the 'not much explored' Craven area of West Yorkshire, following an excursion to the Lake District. Among the chasms that Hutton was led to by his local guide were Yordas Cave (later to be opened as a show cave), Gingle Pot, Hurtle Pot, Catknow Hole and Weathercoat Cave. Interestingly, although he was keen to seek out the 'most surprising natural curiosities' of the area, and although he visited the slopes of Ingleborough, Hutton was not at all anxious to visit 'Gaper Gill', but left it for 'another summer's excursion' – suggesting that at that date the pothole hardly figured on the underground map of Britain, and even local guides still had little idea of its hidden magnitude.

Hutton viewed subterranean Craven very much through the lens of classical mythology. Descending into Hurtle Pot, he imagined himself as Aeneas entering the infernal regions, while investigating Yordas Cave he envisaged himself first as Cadmus encountering the den of a huge serpent, and then as Actaeon intruding upon the bathing goddess Diana.[48] His local guide seems to have been more than happy to exploit such fancies, assuring him that had he only arrived a few days earlier, he would have encountered 'a few rural beauties having assembled there on an occasion like that of Diana and her nymphs'.[49]

Hutton was roundly mocked for his classical fantasies by an anonymous reviewer for *Blackwood's Edinburgh Magazine*, who scoffingly dubbed him 'Aeneas Hutton'.[50] Like Sturmey, his own cave exploration was far from heroic. His account repeatedly explains that investigations were terminated because of the threat of being 'besmeared with slime and mud'.[51] And when offered 'the honour of making the first expedition for discoveries' along an unknown cave passage, he declined, being 'apprehensive the pleasure would not be compensated by the dangers and difficulties'.[52] Again like Sturmey, however, his account provides tantalising glimpses of the early mapping of subterranean Britain. His local guide was able to inform him not only that 'several of the streams run for a mile underground' but also that 'these subterranean brooks cross each other underground without mixing waters'.[53]

Hutton did effectively place the Dales area on the underground map of Britain. As well as having read quantities of classical literature, the Westmorland vicar had also clearly spent time studying the most fashionable aesthetic theories of the late eighteenth century. In his tour of the caves, he repeatedly alludes to Edmund Burke's belief that 'grand and terrible scenes' could produce cathartic effects in the observer.[54] The caves are each praised for their capacity to inspire terror, with Weathercoat Cave most acclaimed of all for its 'sublime and terrible' qualities.[55] It was these sublime qualities that, once publicised by Hutton, were to draw first the painter J.M.W. Turner, then the artist Richard Westall, and finally the poet William Wordsworth to the subject of the Dales caves. Turner painted Weathercoat Cave in 1808; Westall made engravings of that and Yordas Cave in 1817; and in 1819 Wordsworth produced a trio of sonnets inspired by Westall's images of the Craven area, the first of which celebrates Ingleborough's subterranean landscape. By the mid-nineteenth century, the Dales area was not only on the maps of all speleologists and adventurers, but with its first show caves now open, it was also well known as a diversion for curious tourists en route to the Lake District.[56]

Hutton's account had an immediate effect on the caver's map of Britain, but it was perhaps another eighteenth-century underground explorer who was eventually to have the most dramatic influence on the mapping of the subterranean country. James Plumptre was a Cambridge student, soon to be ordained, when in 1793 he set out on a summer excursion to the Peak District. Among the man-made and natural wonders that he viewed there were Poole's Cavern, Eldon Hole, and the Peak Cavern (then still known as 'the Devil's Arse'). Plumptre cannot be credited with having put these subterranean features on the map – by the time of his visit they had already been included in Thomas Hobbes and Charles Cotton's 1636 poem 'The Seven Wonders of the Peak', and the locals were making good money by fleecing tourists for guided tours and candles.[57] Indeed, Plumptre himself had to contend with rather irritating crowds on his visit into the Peak Cavern: 'the lights and noise of so large a party took off much from the horror and solemnity of the scene', he laments in his journal. 'The effect must be more grand with only a few.'[58]

Plumptre succeeded in escaping from the hordes of other tourists, and in encountering real horror, by venturing into the nearby Speedwell Mine. He was led by miners on a two-hour tour through man-made passages to view first one natural cavern, then another. The second cave was shaped 'like a beehive', he records, with a huge waterfall dashing from the top to the bottom.[59] He found the sight 'dreadful'. Like Hutton and Catcott before him, he had ventured underground to experience the sublime. Unlike either of these predecessors, though, his aesthetic experience came hand-in-hand with real danger. Once at the bottom of the beehive cave, he saw by candlelight that many of the ladders on which he had been climbing with the miners were 'nearly worn through [. . .] so that one false step, or the breaking of a rail had dashed us lifeless to the bottom'.[60]

Besides his surprising pluck, Plumptre is remarkable for having produced a painstakingly accurate and unexaggerated account of the precise route by which he was guided by the miners from the surface to the beehive cave. This account, along with the rest of his travel journals, was not published during the author's lifetime, and despite strong hints in his will that his work should be made public, it remained sequestered after his death – first at his vicarage and then in the archives of Cambridge University. In 1992, however, an edited selection of his work, including the description of Speedwell Mine, finally appeared in print.[61]

Curiously, the long-belated publication of Plumptre's journals was not in itself to be the apotheosis of the underground adventurer's writing career. Soon after its first publication, his account of Speedwell Mine was republished in the journal *Cave Science* – along with a note observing that the beehive cave still awaited 'rediscovery by modern cavers'.[62] That article was read by the Peak District caver Dave Nixon, who was inspired by it to begin a quest for Plumptre's long-lost beehive cavern. 'We started in 1992,' Nixon explains, 'working in the part of the mine that Plumptre described [now known as James Hall's Over Engine Mine], looking for a lost route in.' His team finally made it into the beehive cave in 1996, after four years of clearing debris to unblock the forgotten passage down which the eighteenth-century student had nervously ventured. Once Plumptre's footsteps had been retraced, it was then possible with yet more digging to make a connection to a remote part of Peak Cavern that had hitherto been accessible only to divers. That route, in its turn, was to lead to the discovery of Titan.

The shape of underground Britain shifts and alters for a variety of reasons. Fresh surveys of caves today invariably correct the measurements recorded in the early days of caving, when only very basic equipment – a tape measure, compass, handwritten notes, sometimes even a ball of string – could be used. Cave systems occasionally shrink, when cavern roofs collapse or passages are filled with silt. And they grow when divers swim into flooded passages to discover unknown chasms beyond the limits of previous exploration. By far the most common reason for the constant redrawing of cavers' maps, however, is digging.

Cave digging, Tarquin Wilton-Jones explains, usually falls into two categories: 'The most easy is where silt has been washed into the passage and filled it to the roof. Digging here would simply mean removal of the silt. The second, and often more difficult form of digging is through chokes. These occur where the roof of the passage has collapsed over thousands of years, and the rubble that has fallen has blocked the passage.'[63] Either way, it is a Herculean activity, requiring either the patient removal of thousands of bucketfuls of mud, weekend after weekend, with the diggers sometimes even sleeping underground, or else the highly specialist and potentially perilous use of chisel-action drills, explosives and scaffolding. It also requires an incredibly keen awareness. Few diggers have a Plumptre journal to guide them towards new caves. Instead they are led by the slightest draught wafting blue curls of incense beckoningly down a passage, suggesting a hidden opening ahead; by the distant whisper of voices on the other side of what seems to be solid rock; or by 'tiny shapes in the walls or roof' of a cave, and minerals that seem 'out of place'.[64] 'You've got to be able to read the geology,' Dave Nixon explains. 'You've just got to know what the rocks are telling you.'[65]

In total, it took Nixon and his team almost seven years of underground excavation to find the record-breaking chasm into which they scrambled on New Year's Day 1999. For most cavers in Britain, however, the rewards are small in proportion to the sheer physical effort. Indeed, there is often no reward at all. 'You have to kiss a lot of frogs to find your princess,' Chris Jewell says ruefully. Tarquin Wilton-Jones has also known his fair share of abandoned enterprises – digs that became too unstable to continue, that headed back ouroboros-like to their own start, or that ended in passages that 'closed completely, rounding off without even a narrow crack left behind'.[66] And there were numerous false starts and dead ends before the Three Counties cave system was finally connected.

Nevertheless, digging is central to caving in Britain, and at this very moment there are multiple projects under way around the country. In the Dales, attempts continue to extend the Three Counties system further into Yorkshire, and connect it to the Kingsdale Master Cave near Ingleton, which would add a further 25 kilometres to its length. At present Andy Walsh estimates that that connection is around 250 metres off, 'but if the passages dog-leg, it could be a lot further in real terms'.[67] And in South Wales, Tarquin Wilton-Jones remains convinced that there is still more of Ogof Draenen to find – perhaps as much as 30 kilometres of dry cave, with another 40 kilometres of flooded passage, judging by the overland distance between the end of the known cave and the point where its underground waters return to the surface.[68]

It strikes me that the desire to extend these cave systems, to link one known cavern with another, is not unlike the impulse to pioneer trade routes and link colonies that saw the rosy tones of the British Empire creeping inexorably across the pages of atlases in the nineteenth century. Indeed, digging's closest parallel is perhaps the fixation that led numerous Victorian mariners to their deaths in search of the fabled Northwest Passage. 'To cavers, the map is only complete when the area's hydrology has been completely explained by the known caves – when the individual cave surveys, placed together, make a completed map without any gaps in the drainage systems,' Tarquin Wilton-Jones explains. Such an absolute map of subterranean Britain does not yet exist – perhaps it never will – but the cavers get 'a little closer with each discovery'. Time and again, those to whom I spoke about digging described its appeal as 'a puzzle'. 'When you're working on a project it's like a big puzzle. It burns in your head,' says Dave Nixon. 'It appeals to people with inquisitive minds. You also need tenacity and determination. You never know whether you're going to break into a ten-foot cave with a low ceiling, which is horrible, or something like Titan.'

When Nixon discovered Titan, reducing Gaping Gill to the second largest cave in Britain, he was, he confesses, 'delighted to steal the crown, as it were' from Yorkshire.[69] While sprawling cave systems may stretch underground like colossal sleeping dragons, with a prehistoric disregard for county borders and human rivalries, one spur to diggers is certainly local pride. Nixon is a Derbyshire man, and although he has discovered caves around the world, 'it just means so much more' to have extended the cave system on (or beneath) his own doorstep.[70] The connection of Lancashire's Ireby Fell caverns to Rift Pot in Yorkshire was celebrated proudly with Eccles cake, Lancashire cheese, Black Sheep beer and Yorkshire teacakes, as the Three Counties system took its penultimate step towards deposing Ogof Draenen.[71] And for many other cavers, making their local caves deeper, longer or more complex than caverns further afield becomes a challenge akin to the race between medieval parishes to build church spires reaching ever closer to the heavens.

Regional pride is not the only spur to diggers, though. Like the pioneers who named North American valleys after lost wives or forsaken home towns, the man or woman who discovers a new cave also has the honour of naming it. Thus Peterson Pot, in the Dales, is named after 'a cherished pipe' inadvertently left inside it in 1929 by the man who found and christened it.[72] Perhaps unsurprisingly, however when individuals obsessed with hidden chambers and secret passages are let loose on place names, the results more often recall the worlds of Lewis Carroll, C. S. Lewis and Terry Pratchett. In Ogof Draenen, Forever Changed leads to Another World, you can drop through the floor to enter the Realm of Baron Von Carno, and you must choose between going straight on past Knees Up Mother Brown and heading right towards Tea Junction.[73] Explored largely in the 1960s and 1970s, large sections of the Gaping Gill system possess underground Britain's most Tolkienesque place names. Here Rivendell lies just a short distance from Gandalf's Gallery, Radagast's Revenge and Bilbo's Battery.

While subterranean Britain may offer cavers virgin territory to tread upon and christen, however, those undiscovered realms – much like the 'new worlds' explored in past centuries by European explorers – are by no means without owners. While Titan 'belongs' – as far as most cavers are concerned – to Dave Nixon, the cave is legally in the ownership of the farmer beneath whose land it is hidden. Technically a large cave system may belong to numerous landowners if various sections of it lie beneath different estates. However, in practice it is the landowner who possesses the entrance to a cave who controls access to it.

Today, the British Caving Association exists to negotiate on behalf of cavers for access to Britain's underground landscape. In the early days of caving, however, questions of access and ownership often caused tensions. During the post-war exploration of the Ease Gill system, for instance, the British Speleological Association controversially took out a lease on Casterton Fell and installed a cap on Lancaster Hole. The ostensible reason for this was 'to allow a programme of speleological research to progress unhindered'. However, at the time there was a strong suspicion in the caving community that 'no real research was being carried out, and [. . .] that the lid was serving purely to exclude other clubs'.[74] Threats of blasting off the offending lid began to circulate. Then when it was discovered that with the right technique it could in fact be levered off, the pothole quickly became the subject of secret, nocturnal explorations by rival caving clubs. This situation endured until the Ease Gill system had extended sufficiently for new entrances to be discovered well beyond the bounds of the land leased by the BSA – although when the first of these was found, the BSA allegedly toyed with the idea of installing underground grilles to continue restricted access.[75]

The BSA's underground grilles never materialised, but it would be a mistake to imagine that subterranean Britain is an entirely unspoiled landscape. The British Caving Association, Chris Jewell tells me, has sponsored an anchor-placing system in many of the country's potholes to save cavers from having to fix their own climbing gear in precarious rock niches, and in many caves you'll also find rope ladders in place. In the Ease Gill system, fixed survey stations have been installed underground, while in Ogof Draenen, brightly coloured tape marks out routes for cavers to take, in order to protect delicate stalagmites and gypsum deposits on the cave floor.

Such precautions are necessary today for the conservation of Britain's subterranean landscape. It is estimated that there are now more than 20,000 active cavers in the country.[76] So the underground map of Britain is far from uninhabited: if every caver in the country were to descend on South Wales for a bank holiday weekend, they would have only around ten metres length of cave each. Still, it would be less crowded than some beaches. In practice, of course, Britain's cavers are never all below ground at any one time, and even if they were, they would be spread across the whole country, with more than 1,800 kilometres of passages to share amongst themselves.

The growing population of underground Britain is the third and perhaps most important reason why so many cavers dig in search of new territory – and why the caver's map of Britain is continually in flux. Tarquin Wilton-Jones's autobiography, *Ten Years Underground*, contains one of the most lyrical expressions of the power of this attraction: '[. . .] there is very little that can compare with the knowledge that you are the first person to ever see this piece of cave. An ancient stream flowed through this passage, maybe a hundred thousand years ago, creating these beautiful sculpted shapes in preparation for this one moment. For you. Never before has a light shone on that rock, and the sound of your footsteps is the first human sound that has ever broken the silence of these majestic caverns.'[77]

It is this tantalising possibility of being able to tread on virgin ground, in an age when almost all other terrestrial exploration has been exhausted, that still draws Wilton-Jones into Ogof Draenen time and time again, searching for a breakthrough that will radically reshape South Wales. It was this promise that lured Dave Nixon underground for seven years, and some of the Misty Mountain Mud Miners for nearly forty. And it is this enticement that keeps a small but determined mud-spattered army chipping away in search of that vast, pristine chasm that must – really must – exist in one of those blank, empty spaces on the map of underground Britain. We live in a small and populous archipelago. Yet on the caver's map of our islands, it is still just possible to trepidatiously label regions 'Unknown'. Here be dragons.

Major Megalithic Sites of Britain

ORKNEY
Ring of Brodgar ✪ ✪ Stenness

Camster ∴ ∴ Broughwin
Badanloch

✪ Callanish
L E W I S

Loanhead of Daviot
Balquain ✪ ✪
Castle Fraser ✪ ✪ ✪ Dyce
Cullerlie

S C O T L A N D

North
Sea

✪ Loch Buie
✪ Temple Wood

✪ Machrie Moor

✪ Torhousekie

Long Meg and her Daughters
✪ Castlerigg

I S L E
OF MAN
Swinside ✪

The Devil's Arrows ∴

●	Long Barro
∴	Stone Rows
✪	Stone Circle

Scorhill
Fernworthy ✪
Grey
Wethers ✪ Shovel
Down
Merrivale ✪ Challacombe
Stone Rows
Sharpitor ∴ Yar Tor
Brisworthy ✪
Butterdon

Druid's Circle ✪

✪ Arbor Low

Moel ty Uchaf ✪
Bryn
Cader Faner ✪

E N G L A N D

W A L E S

✪ Rollright Stones

Wilmersham
Common
Chains
Valley
Lanacombe

Avebury ✪
● Wayland's Smithy
✪
Stanton
Drew ✪
● West Kennett Long Barrow
✪
Stonehenge

Boskednan ✪
Tregeseal ✪ ✪
Boscawen-Un ✪
Merry
Maidens ✪

Nine
Stones ✪

The Hurlers ✪

Nine
Maidens ∴

| 0 | 20 | 40 | 60 | 80 | 100 r |
| 0 | 25 | 50 | 75 | 100 | 125 | 150 kilor |

2

Prehistoric Patterns:
The Megalithic Shape of Britain

Ever since Columba sailed to Britain in AD 563 and raised the first stones of his monastery on the treeless island of Iona, one of the most characteristic features of Britain's landscape has been its churches, chapels, kirks and cathedrals. From the squattest of highland chapels, hunkered against the weather like the cottages surrounding it, to the soaring, aspirational spires of Oxford, to the grandiose neoclassical dome of St Paul's, Britain is a land of a thousand stone fingers gesturing towards heaven. Only 15 per cent of us now regularly cross the threshold of the country's churches, and yet for many the landscape would seem denuded – lacking in some vital dimension – without that distant church tower peeking through the patchwork of green fields.

But there are other stone fingers, older and more gnarled, that also point to Britain's heavens, a few, perhaps, even hiding in the graveyards or the foundations of those very churches. Some are as instantly recognisable as St Paul's; others so forgotten that they lurk disregarded on the verges of our railway lines and motorways. From the toe of the Land's End peninsula to the wind-swept pate of the Shetland Islands, they bejewel Britain like the studs and rings of body piercing. Arranged in circles, lines, crosses or horseshoes, standing in intimate clusters, vast complexes, or lonely and singular, they have puzzled, perturbed and captivated the nation in equal measure for centuries.

Britain's megalithic landscape is made up of a variety of prehistoric monuments, all once charmingly known as 'rude stone monuments' and sharing in common their construction from megaliths – literally 'huge stones'. They date from a broad swathe of time, with close to 1,500 years between the youngsters and the most ancient – the same difference as that between Columba's monastery and the post-war Coventry Cathedral. As Professor Tim Darvill, professor of archaeology at Southampton University, explains to me, they tend to be divided into two main types: those from the mid-fourth and mid-third millennium BC (between around 3500 and 2500 BC), many of which were originally enclosed beneath a mound of earth or smaller stones; and those from the second millennium BC (between roughly 1700 and 1500 BC), whose stones defined open-air edifices, and which have always been whipped and scoured by the British weather.[1]

Besides these there are thousands of single standing stones, or 'menhirs', set proudly around the countryside. Not all are as frankly awe-inspiring as the 25-foot-tall Rudston Monolith, which presides over a churchyard close to Filey in South Yorkshire, but many can tower above a well-built man. As menhirs were erected over a period of thousands of years – from before the building of the first megalithic tombs until well after the arrival of the Saxons – it is often impossibly difficult to date them. Those that are contemporary with the rest of Britain's megalithic landscape are believed by some to be phallic symbols, raised as part of forgotten rituals to supplicate for the fertility of the land.[2] Others regard them as prehistoric signposts, either marking the boundaries between different types of land or guiding travellers along trackways – on their annual trek to summer pasture, on a trading visit to another settlement, or on a pilgrimage, perhaps, to a megalithic monument.[3]

The oldest group of these monuments includes portal tombs, long barrows and passage graves. The portal tombs (more commonly known in Britain as dolmens, quoits or cromlechs) can be anything up to the height of a full-grown man. Looking much like giant petrified tortoises, with their huge capstones balanced on three or more sturdy legs, they trundle up the western fringe of mainland Britain, through Cornwall, Devon and western parts of Wales. There is grumbling archaeological disagreement as to whether the stones of the dolmens were ever enclosed in soil. In the case of the long barrows and passage graves, on the other hand, there is no room for doubt, as many still lurk beneath turfed mounds. Through the keen eyes of an archaeologist, the Cotswolds, Wales and western and northern Scotland are densely populated by this type of monument.[4] To any other passer-by they look like nothing more unusual than a ridge in the undulating land, yet beneath their earth or rubble banks are one or more chambers built of huge slabs. The largest in Britain, the West Kennet long barrow in Wiltshire, is 100 metres long – just a little shorter than nearby Salisbury Cathedral – its five chambers tall enough to stroll through without stooping. The smallest specimens are just big enough to squeeze through on hands and knees, and when denuded of their earthen shrouds could be mistaken for broken stone troughs.

All of these early megalithic remains are thought to have been communal burial monuments – the local cenotaphs of their day. In the long barrows, in particular, up to fifty bodies were cosily interred together, added one by one over the course of decades or even centuries, until the monument was finally sealed. Their bones were deliberately mixed together, it seems: an assertion of communal identity and a denial of 'the differences between individuals in death'.[5] In many cases, however, the area used for burial accounts for only a small fraction (sometimes just 5 per cent) of the overall tomb, so the monuments probably also had other uses or symbolism.[6] A few are designed so that at the summer or winter solstice the sun shines directly into their chambers, making it possible that they were also used for seasonal rituals. However, bearing in mind the tale that Isambard Kingdom Brunel designed Box Tunnel (on the Great Western railway line) so that the rising sun would shine through it on his birthday, the reasons for solar alignments can be far from profound.[7]

The long barrows date to the period when Britain's formerly nomadic population had settled down to sow cereals and dig turnips. As they often seem to have been sited on the boundaries of farmland, another possible use may have been as grand territorial statements – Neolithic 'Private Land' signs. And since it has been estimated that it would have taken ten people between three and seven months to build a medium-to-large barrow, the monuments were also probably important as symbols of the co-operation that was now necessary to successfully manage livestock and harvest crops.[8]

Several thousand megalithic tombs from this period are hidden around the British countryside – forgotten cemeteries that pre-date most of our parish graveyards by more than 4,000 years.[9] Used alongside fragments of pottery and long-lost tools, they are the closest we have to a map of Britain at that time. From slight differences in their design, Tim Darvill, for instance, can begin to identify shadowy British 'regions' – the earliest ancestors of today's four nations and 86 counties. One territory spread around the Cotswolds and the Severn estuary; another was centred around the Clyde. Darvill can also begin to judge from the monuments' size the wealth of their respective communities: the better the soil in an area, the bigger the monument. So the area around Swindon, for example, where the West and East Kennet long barrows are sited, seems to have to been the 'golden triangle' of Britain 5,000 years ago. 'It makes you realise,' he says, 'that there are areas in Britain that have always been rich, such as Oxfordshire and Berkshire. The quality and texture of Britain today in a real sense derives from the Neolithic period.'[10]

Both long barrows and dolmens have long roused curiosity in those who stumbled upon them. In the fathomless depths of local folklore they were often attributed to giants – dolmens were their houses, tables, frying pans even, while barrows were their graves.[11]

By the Saxon period, barrows were the resort of dragons – such as the fiery foe of the hero Beowulf – or the abode of spirits. From as early as the tenth century, Wayland's Smithy in Oxfordshire was believed to be the home of an invisible blacksmith, who would shoe your horse in exchange for a silver coin.[12] Far more recently, ghost hunters have haunted West Kennet long barrow, photographing mysterious mists swirling inside the damp chambers, in the hope of catching a glimpse of an old man clad in white with a huge dog by his side who materialises in time to salute the midsummer sunrise.[13]

Other beings also appear at West Kennet at the summer solstice. The monument, along with others from this period, is frequently used for rituals by neopagan groups, who leave behind candles, ribbons, incense burners and offerings of fruit and flowers in its chambers. This 'ritual tat' angers some sightseers at the barrow.[14] For them, West Kennet is primarily a national heritage site. 'It's interesting to note,' one visitor commented, 'that you don't hear reports of these people gathering in local graveyards wafting incense burners over the headstones and leaving rubbish in the yew trees. I guess it's because the poor souls buried there haven't been dead long enough to warrant interest.'[15] The conflict is one of diverse interpretations of West Kennet in particular, and Britain's megalithic tombs more generally. At Stoney Littleton in Somerset, English Heritage resorted to filling collapsing chambers with cement to prevent access after neopagans sheared off the metal bolts barring its entrance.[16] For some, the monuments represent a network of magical sites that should be celebrated and in active use. For others, they are the endangered remnants of a fragile past that need to be preserved by proper scheduling and restrictions. For yet others – such as neo-Druid and eco-campaigner 'King Arthur Pendragon' – they are primarily despoiled graves, whose human remains should be returned from the museums in which they are currently housed.[17]

If dolmens and barrows are a contested landscape, then this is yet more so for the megalithic remains of the second millennium BC that are much more obvious as features of the British landscape.

Even the archaeologists disagree amongst themselves about the original function of Britain's stone circles and rows, and few are prepared to hazard unqualified interpretations of them. The stone rows can be anything from a few feet long, containing just three stones, to specimens where more than a thousand stones originally queued for over a mile. They can occur either as a single row or in parallel lines, like ranks of petrified soldiers. A few tower above head height, but far more are made of low, crouching stones that would not look out of place in a rockery. It's possible that they were once processional ways, and certainly wherever they occur not alone but with a stone circle, they seem to be positioned as 'avenues'.[18] On the other hand, many of the double rows, with just a couple of feet between them, seem far too narrow for this.[19] Alternatively, they could have been sightlines, used for observation of the heavens, but while this might seem plausible at the towering alignment of three stones – the Devil's Arrows – just outside Ripon, in North Yorkshire, many rows are far too stunted to gaze from their tops to the stars, while others waver sinuously in defiance of any would-be astronomer.

Britain's stone-row country spreads from the south-west of England, up through Wales, to Northern Ireland and Scotland. The vast military training camp of Dartmoor is Britain's Valley of the Kings for this type of monument, with an estimated 60 rows hidden between the granite tors like files of crouching snipers. Despite their profusion here and in Cornwall, though, with fewer than 500 in total around the country, stone rows are far rarer than their contemporaries, the megalithic rings. For all but enthusiasts, they are also easier to miss (or to mistake for the remains of a broken wall). Although a few, such as Dartmoor's Merrivale, are important sites on the maps of Britain's neopagans – and many are admired by the country's walkers, and have inspired sculptors, artists and photographers – they have never quite captured the British imagination to the same level of obsessive fascination as the island's stone circles.

An estimated 1,300 stone circles encrust the surface of Britain, clinging (sometimes precariously) to its hillsides like barnacles on the hull of a great Atlantic-bound liner. Like the churches that drew medieval pilgrims, these stones attract their own devotees, many of whom will travel the length and breadth of Britain to see them. Of the vast network, a few are familiar to the general public, such as Oxfordshire's Rollright Stones, which have been popularly associated with witchcraft since Tudor times; the Stenness stone circle on Orkney, made famous by Sir Walter Scott; and the huge complex of megaliths in the village of Avebury in Wiltshire, which has featured in children's literature and television since the 1970s. One structure alone is known and instantly recognisable – even by its silhouette – to the majority of the population, though. It is visited by almost a million tourists every year, and has appeared as the personification of absolute antiquity and unimaginable longevity in advertising campaigns for everything from cigarettes to cameras, from petrol to bathroom tiles.[20]

It is the first day of the Easter holidays when I visit Stonehenge. In a week's time, it will be the most important festival of the Christian year, and yet even on Easter Sunday – or on Maundy Thursday, the 'Thursday of Mysteries', when it is traditional to visit seven churches – nearby Salisbury Cathedral will see just a fraction of the visitors who will pass through the turnstiles of this megalithic circle today. We get our first sight of the monument from the crowded A303, the traffic slowing noticeably as a hundred children in the cars ahead tick eye-spy boxes, and a thousand necks crane to ogle this curious roadside survivor.

Once through the ticket barriers, we file like Salisbury Plain's droves of sheep down a pebble-dashed subway to reach the great grey circus elephant of a monument, hunkered alone behind ropes and 'No Access' signs. The drone of road traffic is constant as the crowds circle this trapped beast, never closer than twenty feet away. Amateur photographers squat, stretch and lean in vain attempts to create an illusion of isolation. Within half an hour, most are done with the stones themselves and are in the gift shop, purchasing that elusive and iconic image of a deserted monument, and browsing through Stonehenge hats, socks, shopping bags and tumblers. For most, this will be the only British stone circle they will ever visit. On the whistle-stop tour of Britain, it is to prehistory what the Tower of London is to the Tudors, or the Brontë vicarage at Haworth to the Victorians. Stonehenge *is* prehistory.

Beyond the ranks of air-conditioned coaches in the English Heritage car park, however, parked on the verges of a muddy lane, other Stonehenge visitors are beginning to assemble. It will be eighteen hours before they will enter the precincts of the monument – in the grey light just before the dawn of the spring equinox, the quarter point of the year, when light and dark share the day in equal measures. For some of these hundred-odd dawn treaders, this will be their first chance to actually touch Stonehenge; during a two-hour 'open access' window, the monument will be briefly released from its restraining cordons. For others, it will be a seasonal return to a familiar centre of celebration and worship. For a third group, the spring equinox at Stonehenge is part of an annual cycle of pilgrimage that might see them also taking a storm-lashed ferry to Callanish, on the Isle of Lewis, for the winter solstice, camping at Somerset's Stanton Drew on Midsummer's Eve, driving hundreds of miles north to Cumbria's Castlerigg for the autumn equinox, and visiting any number of local megalithic sites in the months between.

For these megalithic devotees, dawn at Stonehenge – even without the daytime crowds – contrasts starkly with the experience at other British stone circles. Visit the majority of Stonehenge's 1,300 sisters and there is no car park, no bunkered toilets, no gift shop, and indeed very little to help you find the monument beyond an OS gridmark and a sharp eye. When I went to Cumbria's Long Meg for the first time, I resorted to asking for directions at a nearby farm. 'Are you a Druid?' came the polite enquiry. 'Because they were here last week, and they couldn't find it either.' Long Meg and her Daughters is the sixth largest stone circle in Britain, with its main megalith (Meg herself) standing a proud twelve feet tall. The detection of smaller and lower specimens is more of a challenge. Although Stonehenge and Avebury were built in the accessible lowlands of central southern England, far more stone circles were erected in those areas that were just beginning to be settled in the second millennium BC and where there was ample room for these new-fangled monuments – the jagged upland areas of western and northern Britain.[21] Today, then, those hunting for circles need to resort most often to the gorse-covered slopes of Scotland, Cumbria, Wales and the West Country, following in the footsteps of some of the first hardy colonists there.

The sense of being somehow close to those ancient megalith-builders – of being able to 'intuit a little of how life was then' – is certainly one motive for those who seek out Britain's hundreds of lesser-known stone circles.[22] 'I like big stones erected by our ancestors,' writes one blogger on the megalith hunter's website, the Megalithic Portal.[23] Another takes a Stone Age axe into circles with him – to charge it up, as it were, by proximity to its history. The Megalithic Portal has more than 10,000 registered users, and that seems to be merely a fraction of the traffic going through the site; when I viewed it, the registered users online were outnumbered by more than fifty to one by curious visitors like myself. The site is just one of many devoted to Britain's megaliths, or to stone circles in particular. Its name gives a further insight into the attraction of spending weary weekends stomping across heather, compass in one hand, gazetteer in the other. Stone circles are, for many, portals into an alternative reality.[24] 'They create gateways. If you stand in the middle you can go somewhere. They can be seen just as a church can be seen – as a doorway to the other,' explains Philip Carr-Gomm, a neo-Druid and one of Britain's most prolific authorities on New Age spirituality.[25]

Those seeking that experience of 'otherness' often avoid busy Stonehenge entirely. 'Many stones enthusiasts consider Stonehenge to be overrated,' explains Andy Burnham, creator of the Megalithic Portal. 'There is a vast array of equally fascinating and enigmatic sites throughout the British Isles.' A few would go even further and claim that Stonehenge's spiritual power has actually been diminished by the thousands of tourists visiting it, as effectively as if each had taken away a tiny pocketful of rock.[26] Often these megalith enthusiasts have a sense of affiliation to a local site that they will visit with the regular devotion of any congregation. Others will tramp to especially remote circles, shared only with curlews, rabbits and the odd sheep. And for a large proportion of Andy's members, Avebury, rather than Stonehenge, represents the centre of megalithic Britain.

It is not only the roped and ticketed experience of Stonehenge that makes neighbouring Avebury the preferred site of stone-circle enthusiasts; Avebury itself is also managed by English Heritage, and visited by thousands of tourists every year. It is also the fact that Stonehenge's very structure means it is atypical of British stone circles – as much an oddity on the megalithic map of Britain as the Arc de Triomphe would be in the middle of a Wiltshire village. Much of this oddness is because, as we now know, the monument was constructed in several stages – beginning around 2440 BC not as a stone circle at all, but as an earthen ring, or 'henge', with just two large stones standing by its entrance. Over hundreds of years, successive generations imposed their own makeovers on the monument – altering its axis, adding low 'bluestones' (originally from the Preseli Mountains of Wales), then removing these altogether before positioning them again in subtly different arrangements – never quite satisfied with the designs inherited from their ancestors. It was not until around 2000 BC that the great lintelled 'trilithons' – what most people think of as the 'true' Stonehenge – were erected in a circle and inner horseshoe formation. Even this did not mark the end of Stonehenge's alterations, however; around 500 years later, further bluestones were added, and it was not until nearly 1100 BC – 400 years after stone circles had ceased being built in most of Britain – that the monument was finessed into its final incarnation.[27]

Stonehenge, then, probably had a far longer active life than most of Britain's stone circles, and what we see now is as much a palimpsest as any Roman-bath-turned-medieval-shrine-turned-modern-pub. Indeed, Aubrey Burl, Britain's most prolific author on stone circles, has described it as 'a megalithic transvestite'.[28] As well as circles, it incorporates formations of stones – a horseshoe and a rectangle – that are found in only a handful of other places in Britain, but which are common in Brittany. And its trilithons – unique among British stone circles – were constructed using not the techniques of stoneworkers, but the mortice and tenon joints typical of woodwork. Such oddities have led Burl to describe it as 'foreign, revolutionary, and inimical to indigenous styles', representing not the centre of Britain's megalithic map, but rather an outpost of Breton culture.[29]

Perhaps because, with its lintelled trilithons, Stonehenge has always looked so obviously man-made – and also because of its accessible lowland position – it was the first point to be recognised, in historical times, on the megalithic map of Britain. The first visitors there were Romans, who in the early days of their conquest of Britain seem to have wrecked the monument, and then later – in an ironic volte-face – come to its ruins as tourists. How they viewed it can only be guessed at, though their early maltreatment hints at its being considered either as a centre or as a symbol of native resistance.[30]

It was not until around 700 years after this Roman sight-seeing that the earliest written accounts of Stonehenge appeared. The first was in Henry of Huntingdon's *History of the English*, written around AD 1129, in which the monument was listed as the Second Wonder of Britain (the first being Peak Cavern in Derbyshire).[31] Henry – whose information about the monument was probably second-hand – made no attempt to explain Stonehenge. His contemporary Geoffrey of Monmouth was bolder in his speculations, claiming in his *History of the Kings of Britain*, written seven years later, that the stones had originally formed 'The Giant's Round' in Ireland, and had been brought to Salisbury Plain by the wizard Merlin to mark the triumph of the British king Aurelius Ambrosius over the dastardly Saxon invader Hengist.[32]

There are no written accounts of any other megalithic rings from around this time. Smaller and more remote ones were probably dismissed as natural outcroppings of stone. To a society that believed fossils were ornaments planted in the earth by a Christian deity, there was no difficulty at all in the notion that rocks could be naturally geometrically arranged.[33] It seems likely, though, that those that happened to be close to roads or villages, like Stonehenge, were noticed and attributed by locals to giants or magical beings.

Late in the reign of Queen Elizabeth, a new addition was added to this hoard of folklore in the West Country – the belief that stone circles represented groups of sportspeople or revellers who had been petrified for enjoying their pastimes on a Sunday. The historian Ronald Hutton has argued that this folk tale, which still lingers in the many 'maidens' among today's megalithic rings, began life as Sabbatarian propaganda – part of the Puritan campaign against Sunday games and dances. It was first recorded in Cornwall in 1602, but within a few decades flinty young women and musicians were gathering moss across the south-west of England, and then in Scotland and Wales.[34] These tales were recorded in the work of the earliest British topographers and antiquaries. Their wide-ranging guides to the country – the *Lonely Planets* of the seventeenth century – attempted to catalogue everything of interest for each county, from plant life, to churches, to notable families. Stone circles were therefore noted only in passing, but for many individual sites this was the first time their existence had been advertised beyond their own immediate neighbourhood, and so it was the first tiny step towards a map of megalithic Britain.[35]

None of the countryside's merry maidens or devilish pipers were at first viewed as in any way related to the dramatic monument of Stonehenge, however. By the seventeenth century, the origins and use of that edifice had become the subjects of heated debate. Within the course of just over a hundred years, five detailed surverys of Stonehenge were made, each one looking quite different, as its draughtsman's pencil nudged stones this way and that to persuade the resolutely enigmatic remains to compose a meaningful picture.[36] The earliest was commissioned in 1620 by James I, who commanded the neoclassical architect Inigo Jones to make a plan of Stonehenge and explain its origins. Jones's conclusions were published after his death in 1652 as a full-length book, *The Most Notable Antiquity of Great Britain, Vulgarly Called Stoneheng, on Salisbury Plain. Restored.* It was the first book in any language devoted to a single prehistoric monument – though it deduced that Stonehenge could not be prehistoric because it was clearly the work of 'grand masters of the art of building'.[37] For Jones, who had spent his youth sightseeing at Roman ruins, and whose knowledge of early Britain came entirely from Roman authors, the ancient Britons were 'utterly ignorant, as a nation wholly addicted to wars, never applying themselves to the study of Arts'.[38] The logical answer, then, was that Stonehenge must be a Roman temple.

Jones's theory was rudely reviewed and sold badly.[39] It quickly inspired rival theories – for the doctor Walter Charleton, Stonehenge was the ancient coronation place of the Danes, while for the lawyer Aylett Sammes, it was without doubt built by Phoenicians 'from the farthermost parts of Africa'.[40] While this often venomous debate was under way, however, the largest and most complex megalithic site in Britain, just 17 miles away from Stonehenge, had attracted attention for the first time. On New Year's Day 1649, a young Wiltshire clergyman, John Aubrey, was riding with the hunt when they chanced to pass through the village of Avebury. 'I was wonderfully surprised by the sight of those vast stones: of which I had never heard before,' he recorded. This was not surprising – Inigo Jones had mistaken the huge stone circles for a quarry, while other antiquaries had assumed they were natural outcrops. Aubrey recognised them as 'segments of rude circles' and concluded that they 'had been in the old time complete'. His real stroke of genius, however, was to spot that Avebury was the same type of monument as Stonehenge. Indeed, he claimed, it 'did as much excel Stonehenge, as a Cathedral does a Parish Church' – anticipating by over 300 years the feelings of many megalith enthusiasts today.[41]

From this flash of insight, Aubrey went on to survey the Somerset circle of Stanton Drew, once again using comparative techniques to 'make the stones speake for themselves'.[42] Crucially, he also corresponded about his findings with Scottish and Welsh members of the newly formed Royal Society. Since many of these antiquaries could describe stone circles in areas that had never been part of Roman Britain or had no record of Viking settlement, the inevitable realisation was that the whole group of monuments could only be prehistoric, the work of ancient Britons. From this, Aubrey further concluded that they must be temples of 'the most eminent priests (or order of priests) among the Britaines [. . .] Druids'.[43] This was a theory that had already been suggested about a distinctive group of stone circles around Aberdeen (today known as 'recumbent' on account of their one horizontal stone).[44] It was Aubrey, however, who first saw the whole network of Britain's megalithic rings as Druid temples – an association that was to endure for centuries.

Although John Aubrey was unarguably the father of modern archaeology, he was also a terrible scatterbrain – 'magotie-headed', one (former) friend called him – and when he died in 1697, his work was still sprawling and in disarray.[45] It took another generation to bring Druid temples to the attention of the British public. In 1718, after reading Aubrey's notes, the Lincolnshire doctor William Stukeley was inspired to carry out his own extensive fieldwork at Avebury and Stonehenge. Stukeley measured and counted the megaliths with an accuracy beyond that of any earlier surveyor of stone circles, and was consequently the first person to notice Stonehenge's alignment with the rising sun at the summer solstice, and to give names to many features – the 'trilithons' at Stonehenge, the 'sanctuary' at Avebury, and so on – that are still used today.[46]

Stukeley went on to publish two monumental studies of the rings, *Stonehenge* (1740) and *Abury* (1743).[47] In these he not only claimed, like Aubrey, that all the stone circles in Britain were Druidical, but also aimed to make 'the reader [see] them, as in their first ages' by painting in colourful detail the ceremonies that had once been performed there. At Avebury, he imagined that 'sacrifices were offered and administered by the lesser orders of priests around the amber or central pyramid. The highest part of religion was to be performed by the Archdruid and the upper order of priests before the magnificent cove of the northern temple, together with hymns, incense, musick, and the like.'[48] Through Stukeley's eyes, the Avebury complex could be divided into separate temples dedicated to the sun, the moon and mother earth, with the main circle and avenue taking on the form of a great snake running through a ring – an Egyptian symbol of eternal life.[49] The remainder of Britain's stone circles and rows were likewise either circular temples or serpent-shaped 'dracontia'.[50]

It took just a few decades from the publication of Stukeley's studies for Britain to go completely Druid-mad. Since the Act of Union in 1707, the newly united country had needed a common heritage to draw England, Wales and Scotland together. Druids and their temples, occurring in almost every part of the kingdom, fitted the bill perfectly.[51] Studies of other 'Druidic remains' quickly followed. In 1747, the Bath architect John Wood argued that the Somerset stone circle Stanton Drew had been a Druidic university, and a few decades later a Glamorgan stonemason, Edward Williams (now better known as Iolo Morganwg), forged documents outlining the precise form of the Druidic ceremonies that had taken place in Welsh stone circles.[52]

If there was a general consensus by this stage that stone circles were the work of the Druids, however, there was still disagreement about precisely what the ancient bearded fellows had got up to in them. For Stukeley, Druids had been wise and gentle philosophers who had been tipped off about the coming of Christ by a disciple of the prophet Abraham. Consequently, they had worshipped as proto-Christians in stone circles – sacrificing a few animals, admittedly, but only because they had interpreted Christ's sacrifice too literally.[53] On the whole, their solstice festivals had been rather jolly affairs, complete with sporting events to entertain the masses. Other antiquaries, though, had more lurid dreams. For the Cornish clergyman William Borlase, whose *Antiquities, Historical and Monumental, of the County of Cornwall* was published in 1754, that county's megalithic monuments had witnessed the bloody sacrifice of women and children.[54] The hard-drinking, Mercury-worshipping Druids had used drums and trumpets to drown their cries, and at sites like the Hurlers, where there are multiple circles of stones, they had used individual rings to 'prepare, kill, examine and burn the victim'.[55]

These two diametrically opposed images of Britain's stone circles battled it out for dominance on the bookshelves of the eighteenth century. By the dawn of the Romantic period, though, it was really a foregone conclusion which vision would appeal most to poets keen to thrill their audiences with a shiver of the sublime. For the poet and visionary William Blake, Stonehenge was 'a building of eternal death: whose proportions are eternal despair'; Wordsworth imagined the monument encircling a burning wicker man, stuffed with human sacrifices; and a host of minor poets had endless fun visualising raised sickles, shrieking victims and clotted gore in stone circles around the country.[56]

It took until the 1860s for the Druids to be evicted from Britain's stone circles by a new conception of prehistory, which recognised that the period from the first colonisation of Britain until the arrival of the Romans lasted not a few thousand years, but hundreds of thousands of years. In 1836, the Danish museum curator Christian Jurgensen Thomsen produced a guidebook that divided prehistory into three successive stages, each characterised by the type of tools used – stone, bronze or iron – and each produced by the invasion of a new, culturally superior people. This framework, which was first used in Britain in 1851, separated the Druids (who were the priests of the Iron Age population) from the late Stone Age and early Bronze Age megaliths by at least a thousand years.[57]

The three-age system was quickly accepted among scholars. In the popular imagination, however, the marriage of Druids and stone circles was less easy to sever. This was partly because Druids literally remained on the map for several decades. It was only in the 1920s that Ordnance Survey maps stopped labelling megalithic rings as 'Druidical circles'.[58] And it was also because, just as that association was about to be severed, Druids began to physically appear at Stonehenge every summer solstice.

The first modern Druidical society, the Ancient Order of Druids, was founded by the wealthy carpenter and builder Henry Hurle on 29 November 1781. Based on the model of Freemasonry, but using the name 'Druids', what began as a small group of friends had by 1831 grown to have a total membership of over 200,000.[59] The order held its first ceremony at Stonehenge in August 1905 – a mass initiation for 259 new members, which attracted national press coverage.[60] Other meetings followed, and the Ancient Order of Druids also proved to be just the first of several neo-Druidical societies to spring up in Britain during the nineteenth and twentieth centuries, some groups focusing primarily on a search for alternative spirituality, others on fostering the arts, and yet others on environmental action.

It was in 1912 that one of these new orders, the Church of the Universal Bond, gathered in Stonehenge for the summer solstice, representing either the first time the old stones had witnessed such an event, or the first time since the Iron Age, depending on your point of view.[61] Either way, the 1912 meeting marked the start of an often fraught relationship between Stonehenge and modern Druids, which has, over the last century, involved bans, protests, clashes with Teddy boys, curses on severe landowners, and streams of often venomous invective from enraged archaeologists. In the 1960s, editorials in *Antiquity*, the profession's foremost journal, called for a prohibition on any religious activity at Stonehenge, variously describing the Druids who frequented the monument as 'foolish', 'unreasonable', 'bogus', 'ridiculous', 'ludicrous', 'horrid' and 'dotty'.[62]

Today, the Druids continue to be popularly associated with Stonehenge, thanks to the fifty or so who usually gather there to greet the summer solstice. These iconic white-cloaked figures, however, represent just a tiny fraction of Britain's estimated 10,000 modern Druids. The remainder celebrate the solstice elsewhere – at Somerset's Stanton Drew, at the great Avebury rings, or at whatever their local megalithic monument happens to be – with a few perhaps using Stonehenge for the less publicised equinoxes or winter solstice. The largest Druid group, the Order of Bards, Ovates and Druids – which has more than 8,000 members – uses Stonehenge for the summer solstice but, in a great marriage of mysticism and pragmatism, gathers there around a week before the day itself in order to escape the crowds. Those Druids who do brave the masses – as resistant as their ancient namesakes were against the massed forces of Rome – are typically outflanked by a crowd of revellers and sightseers numbering close to 30,000. Many are there to peer at the Druids themselves, others simply to socialise, but the majority go to witness the breathtaking spectacle of the midsummer sun rising over the monument's outlying 'Heel Stone'.

For years, one of the few widely known facts about Stonehenge has been that its outlying Heel Stone is positioned in line between the circle itself and the midsummer sunrise. In fact, it is not. Famous photographs of the sun provocatively kissing the tip of the stone are now all known to have been doctored.[63] Stand in the middle of the monument in the dewy midsummer dawn and the sun will first peek distinctly to the left of where 30,000 expectant faces gaze. The problem of Stonehenge's misalignment can be put down to the monument's long active life and many makeovers. Like a signpost at a chronological crossroads, it points in many different directions: its south-east entrance seems to gesture towards an interest in the rising midsummer sun at some point in its history; the great horseshoe trilithons hint at the midwinter sunset being important at another period; and the famous Heel Stone points towards a knowledge of the intricate cycles of the moon.[64]

The accuracy of these alignments, at Stonehenge and in Britain's stone circles more generally, has been hotly debated. For some – most famously the late Oxford professor of engineering, Alexander Thom – the country's megalithic rings are the remnants of astoundingly accurate astronomical observatories – the Hubble telescopes of their time. For the majority of archaeologists today, though, they are little more sophisticated than sundials, their 'crude' orientations on the sun or moon being no more than a 'simple calendar to aid the timing of rituals'.[65] What exactly those rituals might have been is another question.

Competing theories tiptoe uncertainly around the edges of the rings. Most of today's archaeologists, the distant successors of dreamers like William Stukeley, are rather more cautious than their antiquarian great-grandfathers were when it comes to piecing together the broken remnants of forgotten rites – an east-facing entrance, a few lost or buried axes, the cold remains of a fire. Professional reputations can be too easily shattered on the resisting stones of megalithic monuments.[66] Those who dare to speculate more boldly, though, are rewarded with an avid readership, hungry for connection with the distant past. The lyrical Aubrey Burl's visions of 'the robed priest, masked witch-doctor, the shaman, the sacrifice, the tethered beast, the whirling dancer' accompanying unspeakable fertility rituals fuelled by drink and drugs have won him hundreds of thousands of disciples over the last four decades.[67] Even Burl, though, whose provocative interpretation is based on the arrangement of 'male' pointed rocks and 'female' flat-topped boulders in many circles, is the first to admit that 'to say anything about religion within this vague society is virtually wishful thinking'.[68]

Indeed, it is not even entirely clear that the rituals in stone circles were religious. The stone axes found around Avebury may be

evidence of an axe cult, in which the sacred objects were deliberately buried in the earth – or they may simply be the lost wares
of prehistoric travelling salesmen, left behind in a Neolithic Olympia
where the latest tools were exhibited and exchanged. While Burl
on the one hand tantalises his readers with visions of orgiastic
temples, on the other he points out that in Cumbria and other
areas, the stone circles seem to be evenly spaced along the routes
that would have been taken to reach axe factories. They were, then,
perhaps prehistoric staging posts, used once a year on the annual
axe run.

The figures of those who built the megalithic rings are just as
shadowy. They were either panicking farmers searching for a solu-
tion to deteriorating weather patterns and failing crops, or else
'materially secure and optimistic' artists with 'an exquisite sensitivity
to the aesthetics of the landscape'.[69] On the one hand, they may
have been the respectful descendants of the barrow builders, often
incorporating earlier monuments reverentially into their own like
a new spire on an old church; on the other, they could have been
daring religious nonconformists, the Calvinists of the Neolithic
period, provocatively positioning their rings in hostile defiance of
the old barrows.[70] For some, the circle builders were a newly hier-
archical society, the form of their monuments naturally focusing
attention on a single point in the centre; for others, the same shape
suggested a society that cherished 'ideas of inclusiveness, harmony'.[71]

The ultimate answer to how Britain's megalithic rings were once
used could lie anywhere on an axis, then, from ceremonial shrine
to sculpture park to prehistoric motorway services. Or perhaps they
fulfilled all of these functions simultaneously – not unlike twelfth-
century churches, in which as many chickens were sold as masses
were celebrated. And it is also possible that they took on different
roles at different times. For many, such uncertainty is a large part
of the monuments' attraction. 'With megaliths,' Andy Burnham
explains, 'part of the fascination is that there is no "one-size-fits-all"
rule or even theory.'[72] While there is little agreement about why

stone circles began to be built, there is also no consensus on how long they were used for. Fifty years ago, archaeologists may have snickered into their beards at any mention of Druids in stone circles, but today there is a school of thought that argues that those priests could easily have been the distant descendants of the megalith builders, who continued their rituals right down to the arrival of the Romans – just as Britain's clergy today perpetuate the traditions of the Saxon church.[73]

This is all good news for today's Druids. Philip Carr-Gomm, the head of the Order of Bards, Ovates and Druids (or OBOD), is delighted that the Druids have been restored to the country's network of megalithic sites – though he points out that with documented use of Stonehenge since 1905, they already have a record of association with stone circles longer than the history of many new faiths. For Carr-Gomm, moreover, Britain's stone circles form just one element of a magical landscape that includes not only Neolithic and Bronze Age megalithic sites, but also the holy wells of the Romano-British period, Iron Age forts, pools with Arthurian connections, and even Freemasons' halls. 'We don't worry about time,' he explains. 'Whether a monument was made today or a hundred years ago or a thousand, what matters is that it's important to me today. There's a reality between linear time. I see this layered map. The idea of Britain as an enchanted landscape is a very powerful one. I think it can really help people to connect with the land.' For Carr-Gomm, then, even one of Britain's so-called 'fake' stone circles – such as the Druid's Temple, built in Ilton, Yorkshire, in the 1820s – can have meaning and power equal to any prehistoric ring, if approached with the right attitude, and can be a significant landmark on his conceptual map of the country.

The many megalith enthusiasts who are members of the Megalithic Portal may not have quite such broad interests as Carr-Gomm, but many of them, too, are attracted by the idea that the individual monuments scattered around Britain might form part of a meaningful overall pattern. 'Many people think there's a megalithic code waiting to be cracked, but so far no one's theory convincingly explains the layout and relationships,' explains Andy Burnham. 'I think they were placed deliberately but I'm not sure if we'll ever understand why.'[74] One theory, which will be discussed further in Chapter 4, is that the monuments lie on the 'ley' or 'energy' lines that criss-cross the country like the life lines and heart lines of palmistry. Another is that they represent the shattered remnants of a pan-European earth goddess cult.

One of the best-known proponents of the goddess theory in recent years has been the former pop star and author of *The Modern Antiquarian*, Julian Cope. Cope's weighty 1998 gazetteer of Britain's Neolithic sites was written as 'a pre-millennial odyssey', intended to 'give something back to the culturally dispossessed of Britain'.[75] What he offered them was an alternative map of sacred Britain – a revelation of the country's megalithic remains as a vast, connected network of shrines to the Great Mother, Ur, a curva-ceous personification of the earth worshipped in Britain until the coming of the Romans.[76] Heave *The Modern Antiquarian* around the countryside with you and barrows transform into the prone goddess, Avebury becomes her sacred navel, megalithic chambers her womb. Crucially, for this vision of Britain's megalithic land-scape, though, the monuments themselves are just one part of the story. The rest lies in the lines of the land itself. Long, rotund hillsides reveal themselves as the goddess' pregnant belly. Twinned hummocks seem to heave as her breasts. For Cope, no megalithic site makes real sense until you have turned your back on its stones to see, through Neolithic spectacles, the voluptuous, feminine landscape that inspired it and was once inseparable from it.[77]

Few professional archaeologists see any evidence for this idea of Britain's megaliths as part of the country-as-goddess-incarnate.[78] Cope, for his part, scoffs at them as specialists in 'tiny brush strokes' with no interest in 'the entire painting'.[79] While archaeologists may be oblivious to the pregnant skylines of the goddess seekers, though, many do view Britain's megaliths as just one fragment of a larger prehistoric sacred landscape.[80] Look for megalithic monuments on the Ordnance Survey map of Britain and one thing immediately jumps out at you: the south-east of England seems eerily empty. For Tim Darvill, however, this is simply a failure to recognise what was once there. Through his eyes, that south-east corner of Britain is as remarkable as the vast megalithic complexes at Avebury and on Orkney, or the busy cluster of stone circles around Aberdeen – indeed, more intriguing. 'What we've come to realise,' he explains, 'is that there were identical things made of wood in the east of the country. Picking out stone is so irrelevant that we shouldn't do it. Looking only at megaliths gives a very biased picture.'[81]

The first early Bronze Age wooden monument to be identified in Britain was Woodhenge – once a vast circle of more than 150 wooden posts, each weighting up to five tonnes and towering up to seven and a half metres high. Just two miles north-east of Stonehenge, the vestigial traces of its former grandeur were discovered as slight marks on the ground during aerial photography of the Stonehenge area in 1925. It is only since the 1980s, though, that Darvill's map of wooden Neolithic monuments has really begun to emerge, coaxed gently back into view like a message in invisible ink hidden between the lines of a familiar letter. Since then, discoveries to have briefly flickered into the gaze of the media have included the ghost of another vast wooden ring at Avebury; and 'Seahenge', a circle of 52 posts, miraculously preserved by seawater, at Holme-next-the-Sea in Norfolk, one of the few sites to date where more has survived than just eerie holes in the ground.

The rediscovery of these wooden monuments is ongoing. In the summer of 2010, archaeologists from Birmingham University found what was dubbed 'the sister of Stonehenge' – the traces of a wooden ring almost identical in size to the stone monument and almost within the shadow of its famous trilithons.[82] The media attention paid to finds in such iconic and well-known locations, however, gives a misleading impression of the sheer quantity of wooden monuments that were once interspersed amid Britain's megalithic landscape. Dozens of them probably existed in the south-east of England alone. 'There were probably big ceremonial sites every thirty to forty kilometres, across the country,' Darvill suggests. 'Avebury and Stonehenge would have been nothing especially exceptional. It's just that the real monuments are now completely invisible.'[83]

For archaeologists, then, the map of Britain's forgotten ritual centres is forever evolving, as newly discovered monuments appear like distant stars – always there, but only perceived with the right advances in theory and technology, and even then, always on the periphery of vision. Many people, moreover, believe that these ceremonial sites – both wooden and stone – ought not to be viewed in isolation, but as just one type of landmark on a prehistoric map that should also include domestic, agricultural and industrial complexes. Striding through a thick Dartmoor fog with only the odd sheep for company, it is easy to imagine that the low stone circle that suddenly materialises was always as dramatically remote and isolated as it is today. In fact, the heather-covered undulations of Dartmoor were once jostling with everyday life. More than 5,000 hut circles – the hamlets and villages of their day – have been identified, crowding between the tors.[84]

In a few areas, the mundane scenes that once surrounded megalithic monuments have been painstakingly pieced together. Between 1980 and 1986, the members of the Stonehenge Environs Project scoured 750 hectares of Salisbury Plain, seizing upon the minuscule jigsaw pieces of evidence – shards of cooking pot, broken fragments of tool – that would allow them to reconstruct the landscape in which the monument was built and used. What they discovered was that by the end of its active life, Stonehenge was surrounded by ploughed fields where crops were sown, by industrial works where flint was quarried and shaped into tools, and by busy family homes where fires were lit and meat was stewed. Ironically, then, the twentieth-century projects to restore the monument's isolation – by demolishing a café, custodians' cottages, and even a pig farm in the 1930s – were perhaps partly misconceived, leaving us with an artificial impression of its original relationship to its surroundings.[85]

Archaeologists have not just populated the dramatically empty spaces between Britain's stone circles in the last few decades. They have also spliced and dissected what for many enthusiasts is a holistic and undifferentiated network of monuments. For Aubrey Burl, the stone circles of the British Isles can be divided into three distinct traditions, each of which originated in a different area and at slightly staggered periods. The earliest circle builders, Burl suggests, lived in the north-west of Ireland in the third millennium BC. These bold experimenters toyed with a hybrid form of monument – a cross between the traditional enclosed passage tombs of earlier generations, and a new, roofless model. What they usually came up with was a circle of boulders surrounding a flat-topped cairn.[86] This new style never seems to have spread far from its point of origin, though the second fashion in circle building that Burl identifies also sprang up in Ireland – in the east of the country. That style of low rings – often with one horizontal or 'recumbent' stone in the centre – was quickly adopted across Scotland and the rest of Ireland; the densest concentration today is in the area around Aberdeen. Finally, a third tradition of building large, open rings began in the Lake District and then spread north and south in a band over 600 miles long from the Orkneys to Land's End. The largest of Britain's stone circles occur, Burl suggests, on the far eastern boundary of this area, along a line curving up from Dorset, through Wiltshire, the Peak District and Cumbria, to south-east Scotland – positioned, as if provocatively, on the frontier between megalith country and those regions that built in earth and wood.[87]

In each of these areas, Burl thinks, different rites may have been practised in the stone circles. His second group of monuments – the rings found in eastern Ireland and Scotland – seems to whisper of nocturnal rituals, during which their quartz boulders would have glowed dimly by moonlight. Elsewhere, monuments seem to be aligned not on the moon, but on the sun.[88] Each building tradition also perhaps hints at where territorial boundaries may have lain in the third and second millennia BC. Burl's view of the British Isles, then, is of an archipelago divided up by a long, tilted 'X', his three styles of stone circle making up three quadrants and the megalith-less south-east corner of England the fourth. Today's national boundaries have no relevance to this map of the country; there is, for instance, he writes, 'no such thing as a Welsh stone circle, only stone circles in Wales – a handful of disparate monuments, influenced by customs from Cumbria, Wessex, Ireland, and even Brittany'.[89]

If Burl's vision of megalithic Britain stretches beyond the shores of our country, to see tentacles of cultural influence reaching from northern France, then this is still more the case with Tim Darvill's view of the country in that period. Darvill's map of Britain, like Burl's, is spliced into three. 'By looking at monument-building traditions, with the help of genetic evidence, we can see that from the Neolithic period there were three broad regions in Britain that each had very strong links with different parts of continental Europe,' he explains. His boundaries do not divide the country crosswise like Burl's, but into three broad slices: 'the area from Bournemouth westwards had close connections with Portugal and northern Spain. The triangular area of country between Bournemouth and the Humber had links with northern France. And the north of England and Scotland had links with the Baltic.'[90] This means that for Darvill, Britain at the time of the megalith builders was in a sense simply the meeting point of three separate maps, and 'we shouldn't exclude the continent when we think about prehistoric Britain'.[91]

The megalithic map of Britain, then, is a strange, protean beast, forever merging with other features of the country – whether prehistoric, modern or natural – stretching its extremities into other countries, or dividing into new organisms. Every year, it also increases just a little in size. One of the most unexpected of recent growth spurts came in 2009, when archaeologists from Sheffield University discovered an additional stone circle to put on the map: 'Bluehenge', a group of 27 large bluestones that for centuries had kept Stonehenge company, before most of its megaliths were swallowed into that monument's ever-mutating design.[92] Such discoveries are rare on Salisbury Plain, but elsewhere in the country the remains of previously unknown megalithic landmarks are frequently identified – lying in ditches and hedge bottoms, built into farm walls, or simply toppled and disguised amid a welter of natural boulders. On the Land's End peninsula, tourists today pose for photographs by the 19 stones of the Tregeseal stone circle. Through the lens of an aerial photographer, though, the ring (more correctly known as 'Tregeseal East') is just one of three that once stood in a line around 35 metres apart, stretching from east to west; the other two now present only as undulations on the ground.[93]

It is not only professionals who recognise the traces of former monuments. In 1977, the latter-day antiquarian and 'Blakean visionary' Margaret Curtis used divining rods to discover a missing stone from the Callanish monument on Orkney. The buried megalith was officially acknowledged and re-erected five years later.[94] And in 1992, and then again in 1993, she discovered hitherto unknown stone circles on the island – one from the top deck of the Stornoway bus.[95] Margaret Curtis seems to have an uncanny gift for seeking out megaliths, wherever they are hiding, and she is not alone in her quest. One of the main functions of the Megalithic Portal and Modern Antiquarian websites is for enthusiasts to log and share new discoveries, though these are more often single standing stones or short rows than entire lost circles.

The business of identifying these stones – lone menhirs in particular – can be fraught with uncertainty, however. One member of the Modern Antiquarian website, 'Megadread' (who describes himself as 'often seen wandering the countryside mumbling "bloody hell where is it?"'), asked other megalith hunters recently: 'I know of quite a few lowly standing stones, some only maybe

20 cm high, but in prominent positions, and close by to other known megalithic sites. What I'm wondering is, when does a standing stone become a standing stone, is there a height "barrier" for want of a better word?'[96]

The question is one that has troubled megalith enthusiasts for centuries. Should that stunted boulder, slightly misaligned with the rest of the stone circle, be classed as part of the monument, or is it simply a natural outcrop? This has led to one of the most widely held beliefs about megalithic rings: that it is impossible to count their stones. The tradition is attached to some of Britain's best-known monuments: Stonehenge, Stanton Drew, Callanish, the Hurlers, the Rollright Stones, and Long Meg and her Daughters. At Stonehenge, the Hurlers and the Rollright Stones, it is said that the only reliable method of tallying the stones is for a baker to place a loaf of bread on top of each one – though when a sufficiently bold baker once tried this at the Rollright Stones, back in the mists of local folklore, he found that once he'd got back to the start of the ring, his loaves had mysteriously vanished. He leapt into his cart and left, resolving never to toy with prehistoric mysteries again.[97]

In the eighteenth century, the difficulty in distinguishing between 'Druidic remains' and natural features was felt particularly acutely in the south-west, where megalithic monuments are still apt to disguise themselves amid curiously shaped outcrops of the selfsame granite. The problem was considerably worsened by the 1754 publication of William Borlase's study of Cornwall's prehistoric monuments. As well as fantasising about the lurid ceremonies that had taken place at the county's stone circles and dolmens, Borlase claimed that any curiously misshapen boulder in the vicinity had once been worshipped as a rock idol by the Druids. This may have helped him to fill a thick volume with examples of Druidic remains, but when Richard Polwhele tried to do the same for the county of Devon in the 1790s, things began to get out of hand. Gazing in despair across the 360 acres of knotty tors on Dartmoor, Polwhele ruminated: 'The misfortune is that nature has exhibited her wild scenery in so many places, that we know not whither to direct our first attention. We are afraid to fix on a Druid-idol, lest the neighbouring mass should have the same pretensions to adoration; and all the stones upon the hills and in the vallies should start up into divinities. If Bowerman's Nose, for instance, in the vicinity of Dartmoor, be considered as a rock-idol of the Druids, there is scarcely a tor on the forest, or its environs, but may claim the same distinction. [. . .] we shall meet divinities at every step.'[98]

Polwhele ultimately solved his dilemma, Borlase-style, by claiming that every single oddly shaped boulder on the moor was indeed a rock idol. The notion worked too well in his favour, allowing him to transform whole areas of Devon with no megalithic remains into Druidic sites – so Exmoor, for instance, although it possessed not a single megalith, could be 'examined with an eye to Druidical antiquities' simply because of its unusual geology.[99] Regional pride was a key factor lurking behind this approach. One of Polwhele's aims was to demonstrate that Devon had once been 'the favourite resort of the Druids' – more so than either Cornwall or Salisbury Plain – and so attract to the country the increasing numbers of tourists keen to be overexcited by scenes of prehistoric mystery.[100]

Polwhele's mission to demonstrate that 'no part of this kingdom had [. . .] a more celebrated station of Druidism than Dartmoor' was continued enthusiastically in the nineteenth century by writers like the Plymouth poet Nicholas Carrington and the Tavistock novelist Anna Eliza Bray, while elsewhere in Britain other authors argued with equal fervour for the attraction and significance of their own local monuments.[101] The benefits to be gained by encouraging tourism were not the only incentives for these writers. Many were spurred on by a genuine concern for the careless demolition of megalithic remains. In an 1836 letter to her publisher, Anna Bray deplored 'the destruction which for the last few years has unfortunately been allowed on Dartmoor', and which had resulted in 'many of its most interesting memorials' being lost to future generations.[102] This was a concern that inspired some of the very earliest antiquarian studies. William Stukeley began his 1743 work *Abury* by lamenting the destruction of the monument that was taking place because of 'the wretched ignorance and avarice of a little village unluckily plac'd within it'.[103]

The preservation of Britain's prehistoric landscapes continues to be one of the most important motivations for megalith enthusiasts. The Megalithic Portal regularly organises campaigns to protect individual remains that are threatened by ploughing, building, quarrying or deliberate vandalism. 'An overriding reason to create the website,' Andy Burnham told me, 'is that many of these ancient sites are not protected in any way, and many have disappeared over the last 50 years or so under development and intensive agriculture. Even sites that are scheduled have limited real protection, so our mission is to document, publicise and protect the remaining sites. The more people who visit them, the more people there are to keep an eye on them.'[104]

Regional pride also still underpins some of today's interest in megalithic remains. The sense that these enduring stones might at one time have numbered among the most ritually important centres of the country – the Westminster, Canterbury Cathedral or Birmingham Arena of the day – can be of particular importance in rural areas fighting just to hang on to a sub-post office or to be listed on a motorway road sign. Almost every inch of Britain, of course, has some kind of prehistoric heritage, and to the archaeologist, the era of the megalith builders represents a mere drop in the oceans of prehistory. For Tim Darvill, the earliest map of British society pre-dates Britain's stone circles by around 450,000 years – more than ten times as long as the span of time from the present day back to the first shovelful of earth being heaped on to the site of Stonehenge's circular banks.[105] Precious few tangible remains have survived from those unimaginably vast tracts of time, however. Clacton-on-Sea golf course may be able to boast that it was once the site of one of the earliest known hunter-gatherer camps in the country, but there is little among the automatic sprinklers and perfect greens today to suggest that bison and elephant were once crudely butchered there. At Britain's megalithic sites, on the other hand, the flitting, unimaginable past seems for a moment to be anchored down – literally set in stone.

There have been many heads scratched over the question of why, precisely, we have continued to be so curiously drawn to lichen-covered boulders heaved into rows and circles. In the eighteenth century, Edmund Burke speculated that 'When any work seems to have required immense force and labour to effect it, the idea is grand. Stonehenge, neither for its position nor ornament, has anything admirable; but those huge rude masses of stone, set on end, and piled on each other, turn the mind on the immense force necessary for such a work.'[106] His theory is helpful in understanding Stonehenge's allure, but it doesn't really explain the attraction of the stunted monuments of Dartmoor or Derbyshire – or the continuing appeal of megalithic monuments in an age when vast stone cathedrals, networks of iron rails, and vertiginous glass towers should have left us blasé about man's prowess in design and construction. More recently, Philip Carr-Gomm and others have suggested that stone circles may somehow intensify astronomical effects on the human body, so we may be attracted towards them unconsciously, in search of some kind of healing that is not fulfilled by either modern medicine or established religions.

Sharing the experiences of members of the Megalithic Portal, this idea of healing at megalithic monuments begins to sound increasingly probable. Time and again people on the website described themselves as feeling 'better', 'revived', 're-energised', whether they had stomped across dripping moorland to eat a quick sodden pasty in the lee of a dolmen, or spent a balmy summer's afternoon watching hang-gliders swooping above Castlerigg. There is perhaps a simpler explanation than electromagnetic currents, however. In her 1940 poem 'R.A.F.', Hilda Doolittle – better known by the initials H.D. – describes travelling past Stonehenge shortly after the Battle of Britain. As she sees the enduring stones, her one thought is: 'we will be saved yet'.[107] It is perhaps, then, the remarkable staying power of megaliths, their stubborn intransigence amid a world of frightening change and high-speed living, that so endears them to us. These stony survivors serve to reassure us that in the great scheme of millennia, promotions, divorces, taxes – none of it really matters. At the same time, they whisper – oh so quietly – that maybe, just maybe, something of what we are and do might endure beyond our scores of years. These stones, huge and hoary, low and glittering, piled high or buried beneath earthen shrouds, are, perhaps, the anchors holding Great Britain steady amid the currents of time and change.

Hidden Highways: The Lost Map of Britain's Inland Navigators

Down the narrow 25-mile length of Wales's Taff Valley, the cities of Cardiff and Merthyr Tydfil glare at each other in ancient rivalry. Over the course of the last two centuries, the respective fortunes of these neighbouring civic opponents has reversed. In the eighteenth century, the journey north to 'Merthyr' was a trip to the big smoke. Its fortune forged in the glaring heat of its ironworks, the city was the largest in Wales, with a population of 7,000, and was more than three times the size of the 'obscure and inconsiderable' small town of Cardiff.[1] Today, though, it is towards Cardiff's sports stadiums, domed university buildings and steel-capped Senedd building that the commuter traffic queues each weekday morning. As you drive to Wales's capital and largest city along the hurtling lanes of the A470, the secret of Cardiff's dramatic change in fortune is almost close enough to touch – and yet nearly invisible. Between the southbound carriageway of the unofficial 'TransWales Highway' and the older Merthyr Road is one of the few remaining clues: a low wall whose soot-blackened stones once bordered the towpath of the greatest of South Wales's man-made waterways, an aquatic route almost as congested, as vital to trade, and as central to local lives as the dual carriageway that cuts through central Wales today.

The Glamorganshire Canal, which now lies hidden beneath the tarmac of the A470, was opened amid great celebrations in 1794, after three and a half years of back-breaking excavation. The purpose of the 'Great Ditch', as it was locally and affectionately known, was to carry iron and coal over nearly 25 miles of water and through 49 locks, from Merthyr Tydfil's collieries and ironworks to the fresh sea air at Cardiff Docks. By the middle of the nineteenth century, more than 200 barges were travelling up and down the route every day. This impressive flotilla also carried another, invisible load to Cardiff: its future prosperity, beginning the process of metamorphosis that transformed it over the course of a century from an unremarkable eighteenth-century town into one of the world's greatest coal ports.

Apart from two short sections of canal that are now protected as tranquil little nature reserves, though, there are scarcely any traces – and few memorials – to this great lost keystone of Cardiff's industrial success. It takes a pair of sharp eyes and a nose for history to recognise the low stone wall hunkered by the edge of the A470; to identify the canal bridge absorbed into a pedestrian subway by Cardiff Castle; or to trace the 115–foot canal tunnel, once the regular scene of argy-bargying aquatic gridlock, which is now innocuously concealed in the basements of prim department stores along the city's Queen Street.[2]

The Glamorganshire Canal is not entirely forgotten, however. Its absence continues to be mourned by some as a lost symbol of regional and national pride. At Pontypridd, midway along its length, members of the Pontypridd Canal Conservation Group have been campaigning for several years to reopen the sections running through their town. More ambitiously, in early 2011 there were calls by the Plaid Cymru leader Neil McEvoy to restore the canal in Cardiff to give Wales's capital city 'a little Venice'.[3] And the spectre of the waterway even haunts those born long after it was finally emptied of water on 5 December 1951. The photographer Stuart Herbert, who has photographed many remnants of the Glamorganshire Canal, 'wasn't even born when in 1969 the canal was filled in to make room for the A470 trunk road'. Nevertheless, he confesses wistfully, he often gazes along the old route of the waterway, and 'sometimes it's nice to dream of what the views might have been two hundred years ago, and one hundred years ago'.[4]

The lost and lamented Glamorganshire Canal is just one artery of the circulatory system of canals – 'inland waterways', or 'inland navigations', as they are officially called – that in the nineteenth century veined Britain as busily as her rail network and web of roads and motorways do today. By 1850, that watery matrix was over 4,000 miles in length. Just under a century later, by 1947, little more than 2,000 miles of canal was left, most of that in the form of odd lopped branches, cut off from the system that once gave them life and meaning.[5] The rest dissolved into the British landscape like ghosts. Infilled, overgrown and forgotten, the lost canals were demoted to narrow, stagnant becks; truncated into duck ponds; reduced to slight declivities in the contours of the land; or, in the most luckless cases, built over by twentieth-century roads, railways and housing. They left only eerie traces behind: an odd rope mark worn into a stone wall; an isolated aqueduct towering in pointless grandeur over fields and woodland; an unused extra arch beneath a bridge; a cluster of seemingly inappropriate place names – the Canal Inn, Wharf Road, Navigation House.

Today, though, the lost map of Britain's waterways is gradually re-emerging, like an old oil painting hidden beneath accumulated layers of grime. Every year, it shifts and grows a little, so that just between the writing and the publication of this book, whole new arteries and limbs might shimmer into life where before there was only ditch and briar and abandoned supermarket trolley. Indeed, the map of Britain's canals has grown more quickly since the millennium than it ever has before, even at the height of canal-building mania in the eighteenth century.[6] The Inland Waterways Association, which campaigns to protect and restore Britain's waterways, estimates that we now have around 3,000 miles of water-filled canal. Enough, placed end-to-end, to provide a smooth, watery highway from London to Casablanca. These aquatic routes form a quiet alternative to the nation's congested road and rail networks, connecting Bristol to London, Liverpool to Goole, Glasgow to Edinburgh, and Lancaster to Ripon. Like glistening ribbons, they tie the Irish Sea to the North Sea. And they have forged man-made relationships between the Humber, the Thames, the Mersey and the Severn rivers.

A large part of the appeal of Britain's canals, for those who today dedicate their lives to rediscovering, maintaining or travelling on them, is the profound contrast they offer to the pace of modern life. The speed limit for the majority of inland waterways in Britain is just four miles an hour, only fractionally faster than a brisk walk. So by canal, the journey from Glasgow to Edinburgh takes more than 18 hours. You would need to set aside at least 32 hours to travel from Leeds to Liverpool. And to get from Birmingham to London would take more than 36 hours, instead of just over two hours by car or a little over an hour on the train. The country takes on strikingly different dimensions when viewed from the steadily proceeding prow of a narrowboat. Our rapidly shrinking island seems suddenly to grow again, regaining the sort of magnitude it had in the days when news of Nelson's Trafalgar victory reached northern England four days later than it got to London.

In fact, even these timings for canal journeys are deceiving. London to Birmingham may be a distance of 147 miles by canal, but along the way there are also 166 locks to contend with. Watching and waiting for the water level to steadily rise or sink in each of these is not a restless man's game. Britain's longest lock flight wends its way through 30 locks in just 3.4 kilometres, dropping 220 feet down Lickey Ridge from the Worcestershire village of Tardebigge to Stoke Prior below. Passing through the 'Tardebigge Flight', as it is known – Britain's canal equivalent to the descent of Ben Nevis – usually takes around four hours. 'But there can be few pleasanter places to pass the time if the weather is right,' canoeist Stuart Fisher rhapsodises. 'The canal drops past hawthorn bushes and fields of hay and barley. Swallows drink from the canal while on the wing.'[7] In reality, then, most canal boaters actually take over a week to get from Birmingham to London, travelling for around six hours every day – and enjoying plenty of time watching the swallows en route.

For the earliest canal users, in the days when boats were horse-drawn, journey speeds were even slower (though with cargoes to deliver as quickly as possible, the boating day was probably longer). Sue Day, the chairperson of the Horseboating Society, tells me that a horse-drawn boat travels at just two and a half miles an hour. Add to that the complications of getting a horse-drawn boat through locks, and on a waterway like the Huddersfield Narrow Canal (which has around four locks per mile) it can take nearly seven hours to travel just five miles.[8] This was the speed of life on the canals for around 200 years. Although there were some experiments with steam-powered boats in the late eighteenth and early nineteenth centuries, horses were not generally replaced as the main power on the inland waterways until after the invention of the diesel engine in the 1920s.[9] Despite their sedentary speed, though, the horse-drawn canal boats were incredibly efficient. Whereas a packhorse could carry only one tenth of a ton, a horse could easily pull a 20-ton load in a narrowboat, 'doing the work of 200 pack-horses', Sue enthuses.[10]

Today, only a handful of horse-drawn craft still glide steadily along Britain's canal system. Of those, four are tourists boats, taking passengers on day trips of just a few miles along Devon's Tiverton Canal, Surrey's Wey and Arun Canal, Wales's Llangollen Canal, and the Kennet and Avon Canal in Berkshire. 'Their work is really valuable because they introduce so many people to the sight of a horseboat, but in all they cover less than 20 miles of canal between them,' Sue says.[11] Sue is now the only person taking horse-drawn boats around the length and breadth of Britain's canal network (although the Horseboating Society represents close to 1,000 members, through individual and group subscriptions). Her longest trip to date was a journey from Manchester to London to mark the millennium – a pilgrimage that took her 40 days.

For Sue, the companionship of a working horse and the team-work with her crew are central to the attraction of travelling by horseboat. Using horsepower on Britain's inland waterways today is a far more problematic enterprise, though, than it was in the days when the steady plod of hooves was the constant soundtrack to life on the canals. Grazing and stabling can no longer be easily found at regular intervals. And whereas in the nineteenth century, a team of two could easily handle a horseboat alone, today Sue needs between two and three times that number of crew to deal with the modern hazards that she encounters. Barriers set up to prevent motorbikes from using towpaths are often very effective in also barring horses. Towpaths that were kept scrupulously clear of vegetation during the heyday of the canals are today often allowed to become overgrown with saplings that can tangle and snap a horse's towline. And anglers, cyclists, decorative railings, and moored boats (especially those with TV aerials or wind genera-tors) can also all catch on the towline – or in the worst cases stop progress altogether. 'The canals today just aren't set up for horse-boating,' Sue sighs.[12]

Some of the most challenging stretches of canal for her are those where boats are moored nose-to-tail, in long, stationary flotillas. Traditionally, boats were moored on the 'offside' of canals so that they didn't obstruct the towpath, but with the decline of horse-boating, this rule is now seldom observed. In those situations, the only option for Sue's crew is to undo their towline and 'pole' the boat by hand until they can reattach it: a time-consuming and arm-wrenching process. It's a problem that's getting worse as more and more people react to high house prices by choosing instead to live on narrowboats, without necessarily knowing anything about the rules and etiquette of the canals. 'Some areas are horrendous,' Sue says. 'It's a disaster for horseboating.'

It is not just the moorings along Britain's canals that are getting busier. The inland waterways may be a way of evading the velocity of the country's road network, but this does not always mean that they guarantee an escape from traffic. At the height of summer, the busiest stretches of inland waterway are as prone to gridlock as the A303 on its way from London to the West Country. Britain's most congested stretch of canal today is deep in the countryside of North Wales – part of the Llangollen Canal, which links the small Welsh town of Llangollen with the rural Cheshire parish of Hurleston.[13] In this unlikely setting, the Piccadilly Circus of the country's canal network is used by around 4,000 boats every year.[14]

What draws such crowds to the Welsh section of the Llangollen Canal is partly the beauty and history of its surroundings – nestling below legendary Arthurian hill forts, snaking past ruined Cistercian abbeys, and crossing ancient Saxon earthworks, the canal passes through some of the most picturesque countryside in England and Wales. Its greatest attraction, though, is probably the thrilling and vertiginous prospect of passing over the Pontcysyllte Aqueduct – 'one of the seven wonders of the canal world' – which carries water and boats for almost a fifth of a mile a magisterial 126 feet above the valley of the River Dee.[15] This St Paul's of canal architecture – the longest and highest aqueduct in Britain – was described by Sir Walter Scott as 'the greatest work of art' he had ever seen, and in 2009 was declared a World Heritage Site, placing it alongside the Taj Mahal and the Great Wall of China.[16]

The 4,000 boats that now visit the Llangollen Canal annually make that waterway busier – and muddier – than it ever was in the heyday of its use as a route for carrying slate from the mines of north-east Wales across the border into England. The same is true for many other sections of Britain's surviving navigable canal network, though the patronage of the canals' waters has changed as dramatically as the residents of our cities' one-time-workhouses-now-heritage-apartment-blocks. In the place of bargees and their families, shipping coal, limestone, wool or pottery for a living, there are now pleasure boat owners (travelling in canoes, rowing boats, or modern fibre-glass cruisers as often as in traditional narrow-boats), and holidaymakers renting a boat for a week to make a lazy progress from pub lunch to evening pint. And that is just on the water. The towpaths of the country's canals today are often busy with cyclists, dog-walkers and joggers, replacing the horses that once hauled boats like Sue's.

One of the principal pleasures of the canal network is the sense of stepping back in history, sharing in Britain's heritage, and retracing historical ways around the country. However, most of the frequently travelled leisure routes on Britain's canals today are inventions of the last fifty years. The majority of pleasure boaters cruise around one of more than twenty named 'ring routes' – circuits such as 'the Four Counties Ring', 'the Thames Ring', and 'the Avon Ring'. The first of these to be promoted was 'the Cheshire Ring', created in the 1960s to encourage the hire-boat business, which was then still in its infancy. The rings are frequently redrawn, as new sections of canal become navigable; in 2011, for example, the opening of the Droitwich Canal in Worcestershire allowed the creation of a new 'Mid-Worcestershire Ring'. Designed to be completed at an easy pace over the course of a one- or two-week holiday, these delightful long-distance leisure routes are very different from the vast majority of journeys that were initially undertaken on the canals, which tended to be local trips over fairly short distances. So although the Kennet and Avon Canal was built to join London and Bristol, for instance, only about 12 per cent of its original trade was ever long-distance.[17]

While aquatic ring routes have only been imagined and super-imposed on to Britain's inland waterways in the last half-century – paralleling the invention and development of pedestrian long-distance routes such as the Pennine Way, the Offa's Dyke Path and the Tarka Trail – the watery heart of the canal network has since its very early days been located in the same place: in and around the city once hailed as 'the first manufacturing town in the world'.[18]

Birmingham may be plagued by the echoing phrase 'second only
to London' when it comes to airports, railway stations and population density, but on the map of Great Britain's canal network, it has
always been the unrivalled hub of the country, the rest of the system
spreading out tentacle-like from its centre. In the mid-nineteenth
century, when barge traffic was at its height, the city was veined
like a Stilton with 160 miles of canal, and even today, with just two-
thirds of those waterways still navigable, Birmingham still has more
canals than Venice. In the 1980s, its watery maze was considered
complex enough to require the erection of signposts.[19]

For many years, congestion was a major problem on the waterways collectively known as the 'Birmingham Canal Navigations'.
In the 1820s, the engineer Thomas Telford observed that the en-
tanglement of tow ropes caused by passing boats in the city was
'incessant', whilst crowds of boatmen were constantly quarrelling,
or offering 'premiums for preference of passage', at the city's
numerous lock gates.[20] This canal rage was eased by Telford's
widening of the city's Old Main Line – effectively making it a dual
carriageway – and later by extensions to the Grand Union Canal,
which moved a national waterway junction from the centre of the
city to its periphery, so that today long-distance canal users can
choose to bypass central Birmingham. The new 'Salford Junction'
(which unites the Grand Union Canal with the 'Tame Valley' and
the 'Birmingham and Fazeley' canals) must have been opportunely
located, because it was later mirrored by a major railway junction,
and by the vast Gravelly Hill interchange of the M6 – better known
as Spaghetti Junction – which now towers above it on hundreds of
concrete columns, its thousands of users mostly unaware that
twenty metres beneath their tyres flows the principal interchange
of an earlier age.[21]

If Birmingham contains the labyrinthine heart of Britain's canal
system, then the Grand Union Canal – the longest man-made
waterway in the country – is its contorted spine. Stretching from
Birmingham to the centre of London (with one rib pointing

north-eastwards to Leicester), this 215-kilometre M1 of Britain's canal network shortened the water trip between the two cities by 100 kilometres, removing the need to use the earlier, winding route of the Oxford Canal.[22] In the nineteenth century, however, when the bargee was as familiar a sight on Britain's waterways as an Eddie Stobart truck is on our motorways today, the 'Grand Union Canal' appeared nowhere on the map of the country's canals. Although it was Britain's main arterial route for canal traffic, it was only in 1929 that it was named, after the amalgamation of eight separate canals under the control of one company – the Grand Junction Company, which had originally run the Grand Junction Canal from Braunston in Northamptonshire to the River Thames at Brentford (this canal then became one of the southernmost sections of the new Grand Union Canal).[23]

When building began on the original Grand Junction Canal in 1793, it was one of the first canals to be created in south-east England. Until then, canals had been built to serve the heavy industry of England's north and Midlands. It was only towards the close of the eighteenth century that they also began to open across its southern counties – though the north-west and the Midlands were never superseded as the heartlands of canal culture. As for London, the capital might have been the country's financial and business centre, but as far as the canal network was concerned, it was peripheral. It was only in 1801, more than four decades after the start of Britain's Canal Age, that the city was finally joined directly to the national network, with the opening of a new 'Paddington Arm' of the Grand Junction Canal.[24]

Today, much of the south of England is on the margins of the country for canal boaters. While the head of the Grand Union Canal leads to an intricate knotwork of waterways that were once the veins and arteries keeping industry alive in the Midlands and north-west (and that now feed the area intravenously with healthy doses of tourism), its feet sit in a landscape where the canals that survive are often isolated from the rest of the country's system,

and are sometimes the mere truncated stumps of former waterways. East Anglia is now empty of canals, while the West Country
has just three short outlying sections of navigable waterway. The
south of Wales, the far north of England and most of Scotland are
also all outlying regions on the canal map of Britain. Neither
Northumberland nor the old county of Cumberland (now northern
Cumbria) has any canals at all. In fact, on the map of mainland
Britain as a whole, the many-tentacled creature that is its canal
system is almost entirely coiled into little more than a quarter of
the available space.

There are three great exceptions to this generalisation. More
than 300 miles north of Birmingham and 40 miles distant from any
other canal, the Caledonian Canal stretches majestically from coast
to coast across the north of Scotland. Distant and unrelated to the
remainder of Britain's canals, its purpose was to allow seagoing
vessels to avoid the north coasts of Scotland. Rather than linking
to other canals, it incorporated three lochs into its route, together
accounting for two-thirds of the waterway's total 100-kilometre
length.[25] The second exception lies 75 miles south of the Caledonian
Canal's southernmost point, but echoes it as an east–west route
across Scotland. In fact, the Forth and Clyde Canal was the world's
first coast-to-coast canal, opened in 1790. Its original purpose was
to link the Forth and Clyde estuaries, allowing coal to be easily
transported to the east coast of Scotland from the west, though
after 1822 it was connected to the new Union Canal, taking it direct
from the centre of Glasgow to the heart of Edinburgh, avoiding
the rougher waters of the Forth.[26] Finally, far to the south of Britain's
canal heartlands, the Kennet and Avon Canal can probably be fairly
described as the only navigable major canal in the south of England
– a 139-kilometre belt of water stretching from Reading to the port
of Bristol.

The Kennet and Avon is now the only east–west canal in the
south of Britain (though it was once one of three great cross-
country routes, alongside the Wilts. and Berks. and the Stroudwater,

ost Johns' Cave, Leck Fell. Leeds Cave Club Meet Easter 1932': the first certain record of the cave being explored is from just four years earlier.

'Katie in the Trenches': exploring some of the narrow, mud passages in Peak Cavern today.

'Katie Eavis in Titan': a caver hangs suspended by a rope in the vast chamber of Titan.

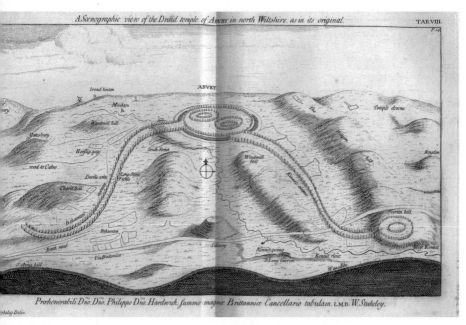

'Scenographic View of the Druid Temple of Abury in North Wiltshire, As in its Original' (1743) by William Stukeley: Stukeley imagined that the monument had been built by Druids in the form of a great snake running through a ring – an Egyptian symbol of eternal life.

'Rollright Stones, Equinox': Cotswold Pagan Society holding a nocturnal ceremony, September 2013.

'Sea Pound, Glamorganshire Canal, Cardiff, 1921': the bottom stretch of the Glamorgans Canal through Cardiff was opened in 1798. It was the last section of the canal to clos in December 1951, when a ship hit the sea lock gates, suddenly and dramatically drain the pound. The canal was later converted into a linear park.

'Glamorganshire Canal, c.1977–8': the derelict waterway filled with vegetation as it passed through Pontypridd. A half-kilometre stretch of the canal in Pontypridd is now one of only two sections of the 'Great Ditch' to be filled with water.

'Stalybridge': Sue Day and horseboat *Maria* leaving Lock 7w in Stalybridge,
en route to Huddersfield on the reopened Huddersfield Narrow Canal (2010).

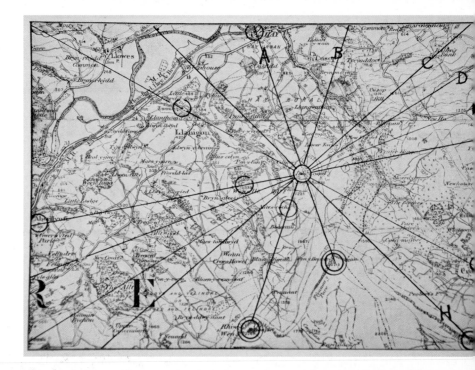

'Map of Eight Leys Through Capel-Y-Tair-Ywen, Hay' by Alfred Watkins (1922)
a good example of Watkins' method of using a straight-edge and pins on OS map
to create lines connecting possible ley markers.

'Members make for Pont Hendre': the Straight Track Club in action, climbing
the mound of a medieval castle at Longtown, Herefordshire (1933).

'John Christian dowsing at Scorhill Circle, Gidleigh Common, Dartmoor' (1998).

'An exact representation of Mr Lunardi's New Balloon as it ascended with himself 13 May 1785': note the oars for steering, and the patriotic Union Jack des

'Samuel Cody, Cody 2E Omnibus, 1912': Cody demonstrates the passenger-carryin capabilities of the Cody Aircraft Mark IIE (nicknamed Omnibus). Built in 1910, it w the first aircraft in Britain to carry four passengers

Thames and Severn canals).[27] In the busy northern metropolis of canalling Britain, however, three east–west routes still race each other across the Pennines. The canalling equivalent of the motorist's Cairnwell Pass is the Rochdale Canal. Fondly known among enthusiasts as 'the Everest Canal', it is the highest canal in Britain – rising over 183 metres, or 600 feet – and also the only one to pass over the Pennines, its two rivals avoiding the range's summit by the use of tunnels. Crossing the Pennines on the Rochdale Canal is a leisurely business. While drivers on the M62 trans-Pennine motorway, which shadows the canal for much of its route, can reach Manchester from Sowerby Bridge in just three-quarters of an hour, negotiating the 38 kilometres of canal – with 36 locks on the Yorkshire side to climb the Pennines, and another 56 to descend down to Manchester – takes around 40 hours.[28] The journey gives a haunting taste of another Britain, where a trip to the nearest city was not something to do on a daily basis, or even once a week.

The Rochdale Canal was the first of the trans-Pennine waterway routes to be opened. Famously, the enthusiasm for a canal route to carry wool across the Pennines to the Manchester mills was so keen in 1791, when the Rochdale Canal was first proposed, that it took just one fevered hour to raise £60,000 in subscriptions to build it.[29] Before the Rochdale was completed in 1804, another trans-Pennine route was already under way. The Huddersfield Narrow Canal, begun in 1794 and opened in 1811, is the most southerly and shortest of the triumvirate of inland waterways crossing the Pennines, and is one of the pole stars on the canal map of Britain for one particular feature: the Standedge Tunnel, which burrows under the summit of the Pennines for almost five kilometres, or three and a quarter miles, at depths of up to 180 metres – the canalling equivalent of the Severn rail tunnel.[30] Even in today's powered boats, it takes around three hours to navigate down its awkward, twisting length. What the tunnel created, though – at the cost of 17 years of labour, 50 fatal accidents, and a price tag higher than the entire route of the Rochdale Canal – was a trans-Pennine route that allowed quicker and more direct access between Manchester and Leeds, by linking to a series of other canals, including both the Ashton and the Huddersfield Broad Canal.[31]

The third of the trans-Pennine waterways – and the last to be opened – aimed to create a navigable connection extending even further across the industrial north. The Leeds–Liverpool Canal was – until the creation of the Grand Union – the longest single canal in Britain. Although work started on it in 1770, the Napoleonic Wars held up its construction for so long that by the time it opened (in 1816, making it the slowest British canal project ever), both the Rochdale and the Huddersfield Narrow canals were already ploughing their way across the roof of England.[32] The Leeds–Liverpool waterway is a very different species of canal to its two neighbouring Pennine routes, however. Rather than tunnel through obstructions or climb over them, it contours around hills and ridges – a grey ribbon threading through the countryside. Indeed, as it traverses the limestone country of the Yorkshire Dales, the distance between points by canal is sometimes twice that as the crow flies. Despite its resulting length, the canal became one of the most prosperous of the nineteenth century – perhaps because of its long, flat, lock-and-tunnel-free sections. And along with other 'contour canals', such as the sinuous Oxford Canal, which winds from Coventry to Oxford, it is popular with amateur boaters today.

Besides being divided into contour canals and those with locks and cuttings, Britain's inland waterways also fall into different categories according to their width. This relationship is probably most explicitly demonstrated at Huddersfield, where the waters of the seven-foot-wide Huddersfield Narrow Canal flow directly into those of the aptly named fourteen-foot-wide Huddersfield Broad Canal. Elsewhere in the country, canals can be roughly grouped into four categories. The ship canals are the vast motorways of the canal world. Built to allow ocean-going craft to avoid treacherous or circuitous journeys around Britain's coast, they range in width from the earliest projects such as the Caledonian Canal and the Gloucester and Berkeley Canal (which are around 170 feet across) to the mammoth 600-foot-wide Manchester Ship Canal.[33]

Britain's next largest inland waterways are the broad canals such as the Kennet and Avon, the Leeds and Liverpool, and the Forth and Clyde, which were designed to carry river boats between 12 and 21 feet wide. These aquatic A roads cross the country from east to west in southern Scotland (the Forth and Clyde), across the Pennines (the Leeds and Liverpool and the Rochdale), and from Bristol to London (the Kennet and Avon – and, in the past, the Thames and Severn). However, plans for a national network of broad canals that would link London in the south with Manchester and Liverpool in the north never came to fruition. In order to travel the length of the country by canal, it has always been necessary to use the seven-foot-wide narrow canals – Britain's nautical B roads – which predominate in the Midlands, where they criss-cross around and through Birmingham with the complexity of a street map. The narrow canals were cheaper to construct (especially where tunnels were necessary) and required far less water supply, but like any single-carriageway road heading into a city centre, they were often frustratingly congested during the height of the Canal Age. They were, however, larger than the smallest of Britain's canals – the tiny tub-boat canals that were built amid the single-track lanes of the hilly West Country and Shropshire.[34]

One of the main reasons why Britain's canals were built to different dimensions was that in the early days, the majority were planned with merely local purposes in mind: to avoid a road where high tolls were being charged; to steer clear of an unpredictable stretch of river; to carry delicate cargo without fear of jarring potholes; or to provide a swift link between a particular coal mine and the closest factory, port or urban centre. The Trent and Mersey Canal, finished in 1777, allowed Josiah Wedgwood to transport his pottery with a reduced risk of breakage.[35] The Caledonian Canal was created to provide a safe route for naval vessels, away from

French privateers, during the Napoleonic Wars.[36] And the St Helen's Canal allowed coal to be shipped to the Cheshire coast without paying expensive road tolls or port tariffs.[37]

The St Helen's Canal is one of a number of contenders for the title of Britain's first canal. More than a millennium before the start of the so-called Canal Age, however, the Romans constructed waterways across the country – including the 85-mile-long Caerdyke, which runs along the eastern edge of the Fens, and the 11-mile-long Fossdyke Navigation, which provides an inland link between the Humber and the Wash. While some argue that the former was merely a glorified ditch, used for drainage, the latter (which was built around AD 120) is more universally agreed to have been intended for navigation.[38] The Fossdyke Navigation links two naturally occurring rivers, as does the Exeter Canal, which was completed in 1566 to bypass part of the Exe that was blocked by weirs.[39] For those whose definition of a canal is an artificial waterway running independently of any river, therefore, the earliest true canal in Britain was arguably the Newry Canal in Northern Ireland, which linked the port of Newry with the coal fields of Tyrone, 18 miles away. It was the first canal to go over the summit of a hill, and had locks, a towpath, and opening bridges. Its success was short-lived, however: it was opened in 1742, but by 1750, problems with its construction had limited its usefulness, and it had to be rebuilt in the nineteenth century.[40]

On the mainland of Britain, the Sankey Navigation (which was later renamed the St Helen's Canal) was opened in 1757. However, although this developed into an eight-mile-long artificial waterway linking St Helen's with the Mersey, the fact that it began life as a modest project to make navigable the existing Sankey Brook means that (like the Newry Canal) it is often overlooked in the history of Britain's canals in favour of the successful and much-publicised Bridgewater Canal.[41] Whereas earlier navigation projects attracted little public interest, the Bridgewater was described as 'the most extraordinary thing in the kingdom, if not in Europe' while it was still being constructed.[42] When it was opened in 1761, spectators described viewing it with 'a mixture of wonder and delight', while the man who had commissioned the canal – Francis Egerton, the third Duke of Bridgewater – became known in the press as 'the canal Duke'.[43]

The six-mile-long Bridgewater Canal was built to transport coal directly from the duke's mines at Worsley to the centre of Manchester, avoiding the costly tolls that were being charged on the roads. It had an immediate effect on the cost of coal, prices in Manchester allegedly falling by two-thirds within a year of the canal's opening.[44] As the duke's prosperity increased, he extended the canal and also had 46 miles of tunnels bored right into the heart of his mines, which today still account for more than half of all the canal tunnels in Britain, and exceed the total length of canal tunnels elsewhere in the world.[45] The Bridgewater Canal remains the largest British water project ever financed by one individual.[46]

Although the Bridgewater might not have been the original British canal, it certainly represented the beginning of the country's Canal Age, and the start of its connected canal system. In the decades after the Bridgewater's construction, it served as a model for many others; its workmen and engineers were constantly in demand; and its financial success meant that investors were so keen to speculate on other canals that new schemes were sometimes heavily oversubscribed and promotion meetings had to be held in secret.[47] When a new canal from Bristol to Gloucester was proposed in 1792, potential shareholders 'struggled violently with each other in their rush to the subscription book'. A few days later, another canal – this time from Bristol to Taunton – was announced; the company was so keen to keep the promotion meeting a secret that it bought up every copy of a Somerset newspaper that had managed to leak details of its time and place.[48]

Within half a century of the Bridgewater Canal opening, more than 215 'canal acts', authorising the creation or extension of a waterway, had been passed by Parliament, and 2,000 miles of waterway had been built across Britain.[49] While the majority were planned with only local aims in sight, a few engineers had grander and more far-reaching ambitions. The great vision of James Brindley, the surveyor of the Bridgewater Canal, was to create a 'Grand Cross' of canals across Britain to connect the main river systems, the Thames, Severn, Humber and Mersey.[50] Like today's motorway network, this would provide the main trunk routes to which local canals could connect. Between the completion of the Bridgewater and his death in 1772, Brindley worked tirelessly on the project, beginning with the Grand Trunk Canal, which linked the Trent and the Mersey. The mission was taken up again in 1783, after the end of the American War of Independence, and by 1790, Britain's Grand Cross was finally complete. It is made up of four canals: the Grand Trunk, the Staffordshire and Worcester, the Coventry, and (the final link to be completed) the Oxford.[51]

For every successful grand scheme of the Canal Age, however, there was also a failed dream. The Grand Western Canal, which runs from Tiverton in Devon to Lowdells, near the Somerset border, is today an amputated limb of Britain's canal system, severed from the rest of the network. Any boats that travel on it must be transported to the waterway overland. When the canal was planned, however, it was to be 46 miles long, joining with the rivers Tone and Parrett to form a great link between the Bristol Channel and the English Channel.[52] The south-west of England had more than its fair share of failed canal schemes – largely because the sailing route around Land's End was so dreadful that there were always visionaries with ambitious plans to create a short cut across Devon, Cornwall or Somerset. The Dorset and Somerset Canal was to be 49 miles long, joining the River Stour in Dorset with the Kennet and Avon Canal near Bath, from which vessels could then reach the port of Bristol. Building was begun in the middle of the route, but before even eight miles had been completed, its overambitious shareholders had run out of capital. Today little trace of it remains.[53]

Lack of funding was not the only difficulty to bedevil the progress of canals. Lifts and inclined planes did not always work in practice as planned in theory.[54] Tunnelling invariably caused problems – it often took at least twice as long as expected, and on the Huddersfield Narrow Canal, where excavation was begun at both ends, it eventually became evident that without an emergency bend, the two sections were never going to meet in the middle. Aqueducts sometimes collapsed – the stone aqueduct carrying the Grand Union Canal over the Thames lasted for just three years before it sank under its heavy load.[55] And leaks were a perennial problem. The Thames and Severn Canal lost three million gallons of water a day throughout its century of active life.[56]

That engineers, industrialists and shareholders persevered despite such setbacks is testament to the impact that a successful canal could have. The inland waterways effectively changed the shape of Britain. Some brought maritime trade inland, creating ports a mile away from the coast. In 1773, Josiah Wedgwood described Worsley – which is nearly thirty miles from the Cheshire coast – as having 'the appearance of a considerable Seaport town'.[57] Others brought previously distant and separated towns and regions into sudden communication with one another, changing the country's geography not just physically but psychologically.[58] The significance that new canals had for local and regional pride meant that their commencement or opening was almost always a cause for celebration. The church bells rang for an entire day in Birmingham when a proposed canal from the city to Wolverhampton was granted a parliamentary Act in 1768;[59] 'the loud huzzas of multitudes' applauded the first boat to travel down the Wilts. and Berks. Canal in 1810;[60] and a cavalcade charged up and down the length of the new Glastonbury Canal in 1833.[61]

Within a decade of the celebratory opening of the Glastonbury Canal, however, the beginning of the end had arrived for Britain's canal system. There were numerous individual causes for the closure of the country's many canals – from the sublime collapse of architecture, such as the Stanley Aqueduct, which crashed into the Wilts. and Berks. Canal, to the ridiculous undermining of the Montgomery Canal by water voles.[62] To some extent the seeds of the waterways' eventual demise were inherent in their own design and construction. Because most had been planned to serve local needs, resulting in a variety of widths and depths, long-distance haulage was problematic. This difficulty was worsened by the fact that there was little national co-operation when it came to esti-mating the cost of journeys that would need to use several canals, all owned by different companies.[63] The narrowness of many canals resulted in dreadful bottlenecks, which slowed down transport considerably. And the high cost of building them meant that, once open, their tolls often needed to be high. So by 1815, with improve-ments in road engineering and reductions in the cost of horse fodder, the roads were already becoming a real challenge to the waterways.[64]

By far the greatest villains in the history of Britain's canal network, though, were the railways. At first, these must have been thought of as harmless enough; in fact, early on in the Canal Age, canal companies themselves often built tram-roads or short railways to connect mines and factories to their waterways, as these were cheaper to construct than branch canals.[65] Once steam power had transformed the railways in the 1830s, though, their potential as serious rivals to the canals quickly became apparent. In that decade, the annual reports of almost every canal company indicated concerns about competition from a proposed railway. In 1835, the Kennet and Avon committee reported that 'the necessity of watching and opposing the Great Western Railway, during the last two years, has materially added to the law expenses of the company'.[66]

Although the canals initially benefited from the stealthy spread of iron rails across Britain – many of them carrying the raw mater-ials to construct new lines – by 1845 the new steam trains were taking their toll on canal business.[67] The income of the Kennet and

Avon, to take just one example, dropped by a third in the three years from 1840 to 1843. This was caused not by loss of business, but by the reductions to their tolls that the canals were forced to introduce in order to remain competitive.[68] As canal companies gradually became less profitable, more and more agreed to take-overs by the rival railways. In 1845, the Kennet and Avon Canal was bought by the Great Western Railway for £210,415. It had cost over a million pounds to build.[69] That same year, four other canals also came under railway control, totalling 78 miles of waterway, and the following year, 774 miles of canal was handed over.[70] The railway companies who bought canals did so either to silence opposition to applications for a new line; to get rid of actual or potential competition; or to build along the line of the canal itself.[71] The unluckiest canals – such as the Croydon, the Aberdeenshire, and the Glastonbury – disappeared entirely into the earth from which they had been laboriously carved. Others were simply neglected by companies uninterested in the water network.

The canals limped on into the twentieth century – thanks partly to an 1873 Act of Parliament that stalled the pattern of railway buyouts, and required those rail companies who already owned canals to keep them reasonably shipshape.[72] By 1906, there were still over 3,800 miles of inland waterway traversing the country.[73] The twentieth century brought with it new threats to the canals, however: first the motor lorry, which roared on to the roads in the 1920s, and then, in the 1960s, the start of Britain's motorway system. Between them, these new enemies reduced the remaining canal network by almost half, as trade jumped ship to the land, and communities responded to the resulting derelict waterways by calling for their drainage and infilling.[74]

The last long-distance narrowboat traffic in Britain was carried down the canals in 1970, some of the final cargoes having included such resolutely British products as Rose's lime juice and the milk to make Bournville chocolate.[75] Some of the broad canals retained their trade, but even these were not immune to the effects of the motorways. The Forth and Clyde Canal closed in 1963. 'It was,' says canal enthusiast, boatman and author Roger Squires, 'the greatest tragedy among the canal closures, because it was a fully operational and viable waterway. It seemed very wrong. Even on the day before it was closed, fishing boats were going through. It was closed simply because the motorway network was growing and the cost of building bridges to take the motorway over the canal would have been so high.'[76]

Almost all of today's motorway system was built in the image of its venerable ancestor, the canal system that still haunts the motorways' progress across the country, halfway between a shadow and a dream. In some places, as in Oldbury in the West Midlands (where the M5 looms over the Titford Canal), a canal survives literally beneath the motorway's feet. Elsewhere – for instance where the M62 crosses the Pennines – canal and motorway lie shoulder-to-shoulder, different generations sharing the same narrow bed. But in many areas, the motorways grew on the bones of the old canals. Five kilometres of the Lancaster Canal was absorbed into the M61.[77] A mile of the Thames and Severn Canal was sacrificed to the M5. And the Monkland Canal is now part of the foundations of the M8.[78]

Fortunately, if the twentieth century brought new foes for the waterways, it also provided saviours. As commercial traffic waned in the first three decades of the new century, a very small band of independent travellers began to take to the waterways in search of adventure, and to publish guidebooks and travel writing with winsome titles such as 'A Caravan Afloat', 'My Holidays on Inland Waterways' and 'Canal Cruises and Contentment'. One book in particular – though not the first to be written on the subject of the canals – was to kindle the first sparks of passion that eventually ignited the campaign to save Britain's disappearing inland waterways. During 1939 and 1940, the young engineer Tom Rolt voyaged around the canals of England in his narrowboat *Cressy*. His account of that journey was published in 1944 as *Narrow Boat*.

'There is something indescribably forlorn about these abandoned waterways,' Rolt lamented in the introduction to the book. 'If the canals are left to the mercies of economists and scientific planners, before many years are past the last of them will become a weedy, stagnant ditch, and the bright boats will live on only in old men's memories.'[79] To many who were already mourning so much that had been lost during the war, this appeal to save a vestige of an older England was irresistible. Two years after the publication of *Narrow Boat*, Rolt helped to found the Inland Waterways Association – its aim to restore the country's lost canals, to safeguard those still in existence, and to promote the use of the waterways for leisure.[80] The organisation began by staging 'campaign cruises' to assert the public right of navigation on lesser-used canals that were in danger of closure if it could not be demonstrated that they were still in active use.[81] These attracted keen media and public interest, and the IWA quickly moved on to restoration projects, beginning with the Kennet and Avon, the Stratford, and the Basingstoke canals.

Many of these projects were long games. Although the campaign to restore the Kennet and Avon began in 1946, it wasn't until 1990 that the fully restored canal was opened by the Queen. The Basingstoke Canal (where plans for restoration were first announced in 1949) saw the first boats cruise down its reopened length a year after that, in 1991.[82] Robin Higgs was one of the self-styled 'modern navvies' who worked on the campaign to reopen the Basingstoke Canal in the 1960s. For him, it was just the start of a lifelong commitment to protecting both the Basingstoke and other waterways around the country. I asked him what sort of person had been inspired to spend their free time clearing rubbish and undergrowth, digging silt and repairing walls to rescue a 32-mile stretch of canal. 'We were fairly idealist,' he recalls. 'There were two things that everybody had – vision and enthusiasm. I was there because I'm just fascinated by water. It's the most fascinating element. And it was a challenge.'

Roger Squires also worked on the Basingstoke Canal. Originally,

he said, most of the work was done by locals – 'people wanting
to reactivate their local waterway' – in much the same way that
the building of the canals had initially been carried out on a local
scale, with local aims. All ages became involved in the restoration.
'So you got the lovely situation where Dad would come along and
bring his daughter and they'd both enjoy working on the digs.
They'd go away tired and dirty, knowing they'd made a difference.'[83]
As the IWA schemes inspired the birth of local canal restoration
societies all around the country – each focused on its own canal
– people gradually began to think of the waterways as an intercon-
nected system. Roger explains: 'People started to see them as an
entity, so they'd travel all around the country to work on canals as
part of weekend or week-long camps.'

In 1970, the Waterways Recovery Group was formed to co-
ordinate the movements of this national army of canal volunteers,
and the scale of projects was able to grow. Two years later, on a
March weekend in 1972, a thousand volunteers descended upon the
Ashton Canal to clear it of the rubbish that had accumulated since
it was closed to navigation in 1958.[84] Initially, though, the single biggest
problem faced by the volunteer navvies wasn't the collapsed bridges,
the broken lock gates, the rubbish and burnt-out cars that
blocked the canals; it was getting communities and local authorities
interested in canals. 'In the sixties, the authorities just saw the canals
as places that could be used as landfill sites or developed into roads,
and lots of people really didn't know about their local canal – often
because they were physically hidden away behind high brick walls,'
Robin Higgs remembers. 'We really had to convince people that we
weren't all mad for wanting to reopen them. But it was a grass-roots-
up thing. That was the key to its success.'

Roger Squires has similar memories. 'We needed to make people
realise that the inland waterways could be a huge asset,' he says.
'The public perception was that they were just stinking ditches into
which rubbish was thrown and kids might drown.' This image was
encouraged by the media. In the sixties and early seventies, a

favourite tabloid phrase was 'killer canal' whenever a child or dog drowned in one of the neglected waterways. Angry locals were quoted, calling for the canal's infilling, and local authorities commented with a mixture of regret and embarrassment. By 1975, however, Britain's waterways were beginning to be accepted as a worthwhile asset and a valuable part of the country's national heritage.[85]

Even in the late seventies and the eighties, new threats continued to face the canals, which the IWA and other canal societies needed to campaign against. In 1979, the Edinburgh Outer City Bypass was initially planned so that it would bisect Scotland's Union Canal. In 1981, a proposed Stroud bypass threatened to block the Thames and Severn Canal – until a bridge was incorporated into the scheme. And in 1985, the M66 looked as if it was about to slice across the Rochdale Canal.[86] By the 1990s, though, at its fiftieth anniversary celebrations, the Inland Waterways Association could report with pride that it had restored 37 of Britain's derelict, unnavigable or entirely lost canals – totalling 450 miles of the waterway network – and that around the country, more than 17,000 volunteers were working on opening a further 652 miles of canal.[87]

In 2001, with more boats on Britain's reopened canals than there ever were during the height of the Canal Age, the IWA could title its review of canal restoration 'A Second Waterway Age'.[88] Since the millennium, helped partly by lottery funding, several further large restoration projects have been completed. In 2002, the Anderton Boat Lift in Cheshire, which lifts boats down to the River Weaver from the Trent and Mersey Canal, was reopened after long-term repairs, as was the full length of the Rochdale Canal across the Pennines. But as well as restoration, there has also been creation. That same year, the Ribble Link was opened. Linking the Lancaster Canal to the River Ribble, it was the first new canal to have been built for more than a century. And 2002 was also the year in which the ribbon was cut on the Falkirk Wheel, the world's first rotating boat lift, which was immediately dubbed 'the eighth wonder of the canal world'. Replacing the flight of 11 locks that once joined the Forth and Clyde and the Union canals (until it was buried in the foundations of a new road), it now lifts boats effort-lessly from one canal to the other in just 11 minutes.[89]

Perhaps the greatest success story for Britain's canal system in the twenty-first century, though, has been the reopening of the Huddersfield Narrow Canal. The canal restoration groups called it 'the impossible dream', Roger Squires says. 'All of the locks were infilled. Some sections of the canal had been built over. At one point, it disappeared completely beneath a huge warehouse, so a new tunnel had to be created.' The canal also had to find a route through the centre of Huddersfield. And then there was the problem of the Standedge Tunnel. When engineers began work on clearing it, the tunnel floor was coated with silt up to two metres deep, and there had been several rock falls where the roof had caved in – some of them stretching for 40 metres. They spent six months in the tunnel, removing around 15,000 cubic metres of debris, before they could even think about starting work on repairs.[90]

Canal restoration projects are still ongoing across Britain. Roger Hanbury, head of the Waterways Trust – the national charity founded in 1999 to encourage communities to protect and enjoy their canals – says that there are around 1,000 miles of closed canal in Britain that he would like to see reopened. 'We especially want to see the link between the Severn and the Thames opened up – the Cotswold Canals.' Roger Squires is equally keen to see those water-ways reopened. 'It would provide a safe passage across the south of the country – avoiding difficult sections of the River Severn,' he explains. The £25 million project to restore the Cotswold Canals (formerly known as the Stroudwater Navigation, and the Thames and Severn Canal) was launched in 2010, although the Cotswold Canals Trust was founded decades ago, in 1972, when the waterways were still being infilled.[91]

Many of the restoration schemes currently under way, like that on the Wey and Arun Canal (once part of a link between London

and Portsmouth) are long-term missions. 'Today, modern equipment makes the actual work of restoring a canal easier. But the
easy wins have already been achieved,' says Roger Squires. Those
projects left to complete are the canals – like the Wey and Arun,
or the 67-mile-long Wilts. and Berks. – that are dissected by motorways, buried beneath factories, or lost under city-centre shops.[92]
The restoration groups remain optimistic, though, and are willing
to bide their time. 'You've got to remember that what isn't immediately possible might be possible in ten years' time,' Roger Squires
explains. 'Factories are often recycled after 25 years, so buildings
aren't always there for ever.'

The Wey and Arun Canal Trust are working piecemeal on the
canal, in the hope that some day its full length might be revived.
Many other canals around the country are, similarly, waiting for
their second coming, trusting to the undiminished enthusiasm of
optimistic volunteers – to the successors of men like the late David
Hutchings, who, after his groundbreaking restoration of the
Stratford Canal in 1958, proclaimed simply, 'Fortunately none of us
were experts, or we should all have known it was impossible.'[93] For
some of Britain's lost canals, of course, any sort of afterlife *is*
impossible – apart from an existence in the memory of local
communities. When Plaid Cymru leader Neil McEvoy proposed
restoring the Glamorganshire Canal in Cardiff, his suggestion met
with a storm of derision in the press, from those who pointed out
that many of the city's high street shops, its Hilton hotel, and its
library are now on top of the canal's former route.[94]

If hundreds of miles of Britain's lost canals will never see a boat
again, however, some new canals might yet be built to take their
place. The Bedford and Milton Keynes Project aims to open up a
new canal linking the Grand Union spine canal to the Great Ouse,
which would connect the Fenland waterways to Britain's main canal
network. This would not be the restoration of an eighteenth- or
nineteenth-century canal, but the final realisation of an old dream.
'There were always plans to build one but it was never built,' says

Roger Squires. Likewise, a new waterway uniting the Upper Avon and the Warwick Canal is a possibility in the future, to fill an obvious 'missing link' in the existing canal network.

While for many the triumphant rebirth of the canal system in the last half-century has been 'one of the success stories of our time', for others, too much has been lost in the process of recovery.[95] For environmentalists, the reopening of closed canals has often meant the tragic loss of marshy ground and stagnant ponds providing precious habitat for plant, insect and amphibian life. This clash of interests has been assuaged to some extent in recent years by incorporating 'off-line' conservation areas into the design of reopened waterways like Wales's Montgomery Canal.

The Montgomery Canal was also at the centre of debate about the levels of tourism and development that should be allowed along Britain's reopened canals, with campaigners like the canal-boat artist Tony Lewery calling for 'preservation rather than restoration', and suggesting that it be reopened not with 'unrestricted access to all and every boat', but as 'a linear museum', 'something like a national park' or 'a full-length historic monument'.[96] 'In the sense that the water channel for pleasure boat use has been preserved and extended then canal restoration has been a great success,' Tony Lewery concedes, but he argues that 'the preservation of the trad-itions, knowledge and skills of the old reality is another matter. [. . .] If canal history is what is giving waterways their particular flavour and value, then that quality must be looked after first.'[97] He calls for 'no place for signs and safety railings [. . .] no cars and no development opportunities'.[98]

The lure of economic 'development opportunities' has often been precisely what has won over both central government and local authorities, though, whenever large sums have been needed to reopen sections of Britain's canal network. So the huge cost of restoring the Kennet and Avon Canal, for instance, was justified by the £350 million that was invested in commercial developments alongside the canal in its first twelve years after opening.[99]

'Restoration is usually driven by social and economic need,' Roger Hanbury explains. 'Putting water back into use puts value on adjoining land.' For those whose main aim is simply to see Britain's canal network alive again, the tourist traffic and the waterside restaurants, offices and apartment buildings are something not to bewail but to celebrate. For Roger Squires, the key to the canals' resurrection from the grave has been their very ability to adapt – 'the world's changed. And the canals have adapted to change,' he says.

That adaptability may well mean new uses for Britain's canal network in the future. 'Restoring canals is all about finding new uses for old assets,' Roger Hanbury tells me. Those uses have already included laying fibreway networks along newly reopened canals so that they now form part of the infrastructure of our IT communications, in a strange echo of the way in which they formed one of the first communication and business networks in the eighteenth century. Another future use might involve transferring water from rain-rich areas like Wales to the parched south-east of England, in place of the fuel and minerals that once made their way along the same routes by barge.

It would be nice to think that the original purpose of the canals – the towing of freight in horse-drawn narrowboats – might survive alongside the most modern usages. Sue Day tries to be optimistic, but in the decade that the Horseboating Society has been in existence, although thousands of boaters and walkers have gained pleasure from seeing her boat on the canals, she has not managed to inspire anybody else to attempt similar journeys. Most are put off, she thinks, not only by the physical difficulty of negotiating the obstacles along modern-day canals, but also by the red tape that she necessarily has to fight her way through before each trip. Every new route means a fresh campaign to get saplings cut down and motorbike barriers moved. 'The admin and planning takes so long. A lot of the time I've wanted to give up,' she says. As rail travel becomes more expensive and Britain attempts to reduce the congestion on its roads, though, perhaps there is a hope that non-perishable freight could begin to make a welcome return to the canals – and that one day, as businesses struggle to reduce their carbon footprints, the plod of Sue's horse's hooves might not echo so lonesomely along the towpaths.

Road congestion and pollution, economic regeneration, and retaining an important part of Britain's heritage are all important motives for wanting to reinstate as many as possible of the country's canals, and to cherish and safeguard those that have been restored for future generations. Perhaps the most compelling reason for opening up and protecting the canal network of Britain, though, is that those waterways, as they quietly thread their way through our cities, past our industrial centres, and beneath our motorway junctions, form one of the country's greatest parks. Not all canal enthusiasts may agree with Tony Lewery's vision of a 'linear museum', but time and again I have come across the canals described as a 'linear park'. They are, says Roger Squires, 'green fingers' reaching across Britain.

One of the uncanny qualities of many of the country's canals is their mutability – the speed with which they switch character, one minute passing plastic herons in neatly tended gardens, then stealing past barbed wire and the smashed blind windows of warehouses, before suddenly and dramatically bursting out on to open marshes alive with the piping call of oystercatchers.[100] However, even in the most developed and built-up areas, canals (although man-made and often industrial in origin) somehow seldom feel entirely urban. Passing through the busy commercial centre of Olton on the Grand Union Canal, all you see from the water, rhapsodises canoeist Stuart Fisher, is 'trees, bluebells and red campion'.[101] In industrial Birmingham, in curious juxtaposition to the scrapyards and brick factories, 'brimstone, peacock and orange tip butterflies' add 'flashes of colour' to the canal.

Somehow, Britain's canals have an almost magical ability to redraw the map of the urban and the rural, blurring city boundaries by carrying with them into the heart of our industrial and commercial centres a reminder of whispering woodland, a memento of fragrant meadows. At a time when alterations to planning laws threaten more and more of our countryside, and our green spaces look doomed to shrink in the coming decades, it is worth taking heart from the fact that there is a hidden countryside along our thousands of miles of rescued canal, which we should value and cherish – and which can often be found within a kingfisher's swoop of our office blocks.

Major Leylines of Britain

ORKNEY

Inverhope

LEWIS

Inverness

Towie Castle

Terperdie
Castle

SCOTLAND

North
Sea

THE BELINUS LINE

Carlisle

ISLE
OF
MAN

Aydon
Castle

Ravensworth
Castle

12 Little Mountain – Little Hill
13 Great Doward Camp
    – Wall Hills Camp
14 Malvern – Brailes
15 Radway Church
    – Chipping Norton Church
16 Arbury Camp – The Rollright Stones
17 Tup Low – St Bertram's Well
18 Arbor Low – The Wishing Stone
19 Bardon Hill – Burrough Hill
20 Connington Church
    – The Chantry entrenchments
21 Narborough – Happisburg
22 Vinefields – Devil's Punch Bowl
23 Wallbury Camp – St Osyths Priory
24 Minster-in-Thanet Church
    – Shorncliff Camp
25 St George's Hill – Chigwell Row
26 Pall Mall – Shoreditch
27 Hendon Church – Lee Clump
28 Beacon Hill – Sinodun Hill
29 Little Hinton village
    – Great Haseley Church
30 Harewood Peak – Deane Church
31 Tumulus on Durrington Down
    – Frankenbury Camp
32 Castle Ditches – Cow Down tumuli
33 Tolpuddle Church – White Hill
34 Glastonbury Tor – Stockland Bristol
    Church (to the coast)
35 Drizzlecombe
    – Moretonhampstead Church
36 St Agnes Beacon
    – Grampound Road Station
37 Men-an-Tol – Castle-an-Dinas

1   Moel Wnion – Moelfre
2   Vale Crucis Abbey – Tushingham-
    cum-Grindley Church
3   Castleshaw Roman camp
    – Hawkestone Park
4   Lord's Hill – Buildwass Abbey
5   Tyn-Green Castle Camp
    – Cusop Church
6   Birley Hill – Pen-y-Gader
7   Dinedor Camp – Ivington Camp
8   Croft Ambury
    – Stretton Grandison
9   Stanford Bridge
    – Stoulton Church
10 Brecon Beacon – Twyn-alt-Cefn
11 Chwarel-y-Fan – Garway Church

ENGLAND

Birmingham

Croft
Ambury

WALES

Hereford
Cathedral

Dinedor
Camp

Worcester
Cathedral

The Rollright
Stones

Bury St
Edmund's

Royston

Hopto
on-Se

Avebury

Glastonbury Tor

——— Long-distance leys
——— Alfred Watkins' leys
------- Other selected leys

THE ST MICHAEL LINE

St Paul's
Cathedral

Winchester

Lee-on-Solent

Brentor

The Hurlers

Stonehenge

Carn Lês Boel

St Michael's
Mount

0   20   40   60   80   100 mile
0 25   50   75 100 125 150 kilomet

4

Lines Across the Landscape:
The Ley Hunter's Map of Britain

It is a clear, bright Saturday afternoon in March. Across the length and breadth of Britain, more than six million television sets are switched on, as the England and Wales rugby teams begin to warm up in Cardiff's Millennium Stadium.[1] As Britain's four nations of spectators settle on to sofas, the country's 5,000-mile circulatory system surges with energy, its veins and arteries throbbing as power transfers from the eerie white edifices of Scotland's Torness nuclear power station, from the vast chimneys of Yorkshire's Drax, and from the crashing waters of Wales's Dinorwig to the ever-hungry cities of southern England.[2]

As you travel on Britain's railways or motorways, the vast cat's-cradle of buzzing, deadly wires that feed the country's kettles and televisions is so omnipresent that you might be forgiven for thinking you were being stalked. Held aloft by a race of 22,000 iron giants that straddle hedges, dwarf homes, and march unswervingly through fields of wheat and barley, it stretches above the country like the strings of a thousand monstrous violins. And for much of the late twentieth century, it really was inescapable, forming a nationwide lattice through which the sky was almost always viewed.

Today, Britain's frowning legion of pylons has been beaten back from many of our town centres and from some of the most beautiful rural areas. They have disappeared from Cumbrian valleys and

London boroughs, their lethal load of buzzing cables safely buried beneath springing heather and suburban streets. Even where it is invisible, though, the National Grid can never be entirely forgotten. Whenever one side of a street is plunged into sudden darkness, we are reminded of the intricate maze of capillaries that feeds each of our homes. And the pulse of this vast organism is constantly monitored – as a million kettles are boiled, the immediate flick of a switch in a control room sends water tumbling through dams to flood the depleted network with additional energy.

The cables that supply our modern electrical appliances are perhaps not the only 'power lines' hidden beneath our pavements and gardens, however. As England scores a try and cheering voices cascade out of the windows of pubs in central Hereford, I make my way to the city's greatest landmark, its eleventh-century cathedral, and up the 218 winding steps to the top of its central tower, from where the horizon stretches for miles in every direction. With a folded OS map clutched in one hand and a compass in the other, I peer out over the rooftops. To the south-east I can pick out the wooded rise of Dinedor Camp, an Iron Age hill fort. In precisely the opposite direction, north-west, is the sharp spire of Hereford's All Saints church. Further north is another tree-crowned hill fort, Ivington Camp. And in a perfectly straight line between that and us is the spire of St Peter's church in the village of Pipe and Lyde, and the low tower of Holmer church.

The lines that my eyes are following, my guidebook tells me, are not just lines of sight or accidental linear arrangements, destined to please the sensibilities of landscape painters and photographers. These prehistoric sites and early churches are believed by many to mark the route of something as well hidden as the power cables supplying the ancient cathedral's modern lighting. Some people call them 'energy lines'. Others have described such alignments as 'dragon paths', 'fairy roads', or 'geomantic corridors'. But for more than 90 years, they have most commonly been known as 'ley lines'. They run, any ley hunter will tell you, dead straight, and can be found in every part of the country. They are believed to stretch from Clwyd to Chester; to cross the Yorkshire moors and the centre of Tamworth; and to link Big Ben with St Paul's Cathedral and Moorgate station.[3] Their uncompromising march across the country might join together Oxford churches, Dartmoor megaliths or London crossroads. Nobody is sure how wide they are – perhaps just a few metres across; maybe broad enough to, snake-like, swallow an entire church. And their length varies anywhere from just two miles long to literally hundreds.[4]

Britain's network of ley lines is now the subject of dozens of books, while every weekend their course is tracked like seams of gold or oil by an ardent community of ley hunters. Nevertheless, they remain shrouded in mystery and uncertainty. It's hard to estimate, for a start, just how many ley hunters there are in Britain today. Although there are two national organisations – the Society of Ley-Hunters and the Network of Ley-Hunters – for many people, following ley lines is a solitary and intensely personal mission, often carried out in remote areas and in the dew-laden early hours of the day. Likewise, although most modern questers agree that ley lines can have a profound and positive effect on us, even among their most devoted surveyors there is little consensus about precisely what constitutes one, why they are there, or how they got there in the first place. Some ley hunters will tell you that the currents travelling along leys are electromagnetic; others that they carry some kind of indefinable 'earth energy' or cosmic power; yet others that the ley system is a means of transmitting thoughts – a 'telepathic telephone service'.[5] 'Ask a dozen people what leys are and you will probably be treated to a dozen different answers,' shrugs the London ley hunter Christopher Street.[6]

When Britain's ley lines were first discovered (or perhaps rediscovered), their interpretation was far more prosaic than many of the beliefs held about them today. Alfred Watkins was 66 years old in 1921 when he coined the term 'ley'. He was a successful businessman, a magistrate, a committee member of his local antiquarian society, and a renowned photographer who had invented and then manufactured his own light meter.[7] He was, on the face of it, not the most likely candidate to be struck by the sort of revelation that would eventually lead generations of dowsers, psychics and UFO enthusiasts on spiritual quests the length and breadth of the country. However, he was also a man who spent long hours outdoors, riding across the countryside to represent his family's brewing and milling businesses.[8] And as his haunting photographs still bear witness, he had a keen eye for pattern and shape in the landscape. These factors no doubt contributed to the 'rush of images' that suddenly came to him on a visit to Blackwardine in Herefordshire. As he later told the members of the Woolhope Naturalists' Field Club (his local antiquarian group), the trip led him to note on the map '[. . .] a straight line starting from Croft Ambury, lying on parts of Croft Lane [. . .] over hill points, through Blackwardine, over Risbury Camp, and through the high ground at Stretton Grandison, where I surmise a Roman station.'[9]

For Watkins, unlike many later ley hunters, the straight line he discovered linking high ground and prehistoric sites had nothing to do with earth energy or electromagnetism; its explanation was more mundane. 'Presume a primitive people [. . .] wanting a few necessities (as salt, flint flakes, and, later on, metals) only to be had from a distance,' he proposed. 'The shortest way to such a distant point was a straight line.'[10] These tracks were created, he argued, by sighting, initially from hilltop to hilltop, but later using a range of additional natural and artificial midway points to keep his prehistoric businessmen on the straight and narrow: ponds, trees, earthworks, standing stones and so on. In time these sites became 'objects of interest, superstition, and genuine veneration', resulting in the building of stone circles, barrows, and eventually castles and churches along ley lines. Although the ley system had been long forgotten by the 1920s, therefore, the routes of leys could still be discovered by tracing the alignment of buildings.

After his initial revelation, Watkins went on to unearth other ley lines – 'more than a score' going through Hereford, and so many passing through one local Iron Age fort (Capler Camp) as to make it 'the Clapham Junction of ancient trackways in that district'.[11] Indeed, he surprised himself by the 'enormous' number that he found and later that year presented his findings to the public – first as a paper read to the Woolhope Club, and later as a short booklet, *Early British Trackways*.[12]

Watkins clearly imagined that in the future, teams of ley hunters would piece together a nationwide ley map of Britain as a collaborative quest. In *Early British Trackways* he envisaged 'a Scout Master of the future, out ley hunting with the elder boys of his troup'. He invited his readers to make their own deductions,[13] giving them precise instructions for discovering new ley lines. Taking a range of prehistoric earthworks as a starting point, would-be ley hunters were to '[. . .] add to them all ancient churches, all moats and ponds, all castles (even castle farms), all wayside crosses, all cross roads or junctions which bear a place name, all ancient stones bearing a name, all traditional trees (such as gospel oaks) marked on maps, and all legendary wells. Make a small ring around each on a map. Stick a steel pin on the site of an undoubted sighting point, place a straight edge against it, and move it round until several (not less than four) of the objects named and marked come exactly in line. You will then find on that line fragments here and there of ancient roads and footpaths, also small bits of modern roads conforming to it. Extend the line into adjoining maps, and [. . .] it will usually terminate at both ends in a natural hill or mountain peak.'[14]

In his later writings, Watkins fleshed out these ideas further, creating a system in which each type of ley marker received a score as an indication of its reliability. So whereas prehistoric earthworks scored a full point, churches (being built much later) received only three-quarters of a point. Circular moats were high on the list with a full point; square moats near the bottom with a poor quarter point. The route of a ley was only certain if it scored a total of at least five.[15] Finding your ley on a map was only the beginning, though. Watkins' disciples were also required to put in sufficient legwork. 'Map observations are quite insufficient [. . .] actual sighting trials on the spot are indispensable,' he insisted, promising that 'if you travel along the actual sighting line you will find fragments of the road showing as a straight trench in untilled land'.[16]

Today, Watkins' use of sites built centuries (or indeed millennia) apart is one of the main points on which his ideas are attacked. It presupposes that the same sites evolved their use through prehistory and history – stone circles mutating into churches, processional avenues becoming the tree-lined drives of country estates, medieval castles springing up on prehistoric mounds. This, as Tom Williamson and Liz Bellamy have argued in their academic investigation *Ley Lines in Question*, is all impossible to prove.[17] Critics today also point out that Watkins' ley lines march blindly up and down mountainsides, straight through bogs, and directly across rivers – hardly the easiest routes for the prehistoric traders carrying salt, flints and pottery whom the father of ley theory had imagined travelling on the tracks.[18]

Watkins himself faced criticisms of this sort in the 1920s when his ideas were first published. He responded by arguing firstly that his Neolithic businessmen had possessed 'the peculiar physique suited to a mountain-side climb' (a level of stamina that had then been lost with the development of pastoral lifestyles), and later on that the leys were only optical lines in any case: 'the man walking on a ley had to walk for the next mark-point: he might make a departure to avoid a precipice, a marsh, the bend of a river, but when he was over he had to get back to a mark-point on the ley'.[19]

Such explanations were insufficient to prevent contributors to the archaeological journal *Antiquity* from condemning Watkins as a 'quack' who was 'ignorant of the first principles of the science of archaeology'.[20] Among the general public of the 1920s, though, the initial reaction to ley theory was enthusiastic. The artist and novelist Donald Maxwell likened Watkins' censure at the hands of archaeologists to the denunciation of Galileo.[21] The BBC recommended *Early British Trackways* as interesting reading for the young audience of its *Explorations at Home* radio programme. And when *Early British Trackways* was fleshed out into a full-length book, *The Old Straight Track,* in 1925, the vast majority of newspaper reviewers were very complimentary.[22]

There were several reasons why ley hunting particularly appealed to the British public in the 1920s. To begin with, there was the question of national pride in the wake of the Great War. Here, Watkins promised, was proof that the Romans hadn't 'found British road communication so feeble and incoherent that they made a new beginning in the matter'.[23] They had simply appropriated a native road system that was already thousands of years old. The contemporary rediscovery of Britain's modern roads also fed into the fascination with leys. For much of the nineteenth century, the main road network in Britain had lain neglected, eclipsed by the railways. With the start of the twentieth century came a rediscovery of roads, first by hikers and cyclists, and eventually by motorists, partly driven by a romantic sense of connecting with the past.[24] Roads, wrote Hilaire Belloc in his 1904 history of the Pilgrims' Way, were 'primal' – inherited from 'the earliest of our race'.[25]

Finally, the mud, hills and heather inherent to ley hunting made it an irresistible pursuit at a time when the Ramblers Association was flourishing and walking for pleasure was reaching epidemic proportions. Vita Sackville-West proclaimed in a review that she could 'imagine no more entertaining way of spending a summer holiday' than by ley hunting.[26] And in the first issue of *The Hiker and Camper* magazine, one correspondent was portrayed reading Watkins' *Ley Hunter's Manual* as a pleasant way of whiling away campsite evenings.[27] Ley hunting held out the promise of adventure and genuine discovery at a time when the British Empire's cartographers seemed to have filled in all of the seductive blanks on the map. Describing his own ley hunting experiences, Donald Maxwell professed that 'every one of our party of intrepid explorers felt a spiritual kinship with Christopher Columbus'. And in the Boy Scout newsletter, *The Scouter*, ley hunting was described as having 'the power to turn any country walk into a thrilling adventure'.[28]

Enthusiasm for the great outdoors was probably one of the factors that, by 1927, led to the foundation of Britain's first ley hunters' club: the Straight Track Club. A small, affluent society (one of its members, a Miss Woods, went ley hunting with her chauffeur), its object was to share discoveries about leys from different parts of the country and to collaboratively put together the first ley map of Britain. The club held annual get-togethers in a range of locations – Hereford in 1933, Salisbury in 1934, Exeter the following year. Its main activity, though, was the exchange of written papers by post. Individuals would write up their discoveries or theories; a 'portfolio' of these would be sent from member to member; and comments would be added by each.[29] The fruits of their work can be seen in Watkins' second full-length book, *The Ley Hunter's Manual*, which includes descriptions of ley lines contributed by 17 correspondents from across the country.

Watkins remained chairman of the Straight Track Club until his death in 1935. Even from the early years of the club, however, he struggled to restrain its members from developing their own interpretations of ley lines – which were rather different from his own vision of simple traders' routes.[30] By the time the club's second portfolio of papers was circulating in 1927, members were already speculating that the origin of ley lines might lie in a mystical lost kingdom, Atlantis.[31] Others were soon writing reports that birds and animals seemed to migrate along ley lines, or that the lines formed part of a sacred geometrical pattern, laid down for religious purposes.[32] And by 1936, writers such as the occultist Dion Fortune were describing Watkins' discovery as 'lines of force between the power centres'.[33]

Today there are still ley hunters who stick to Watkins' original interpretation of ley lines. Anthony Poulton-Smith, who has mapped the ley lines of the Midlands, insists that his 'only acceptance of leys is the same as the man who named them, Alfred

Watkins [. . . they were] created to provide safe passage from one hill fort to another'.[34] Many more ley hunters now, though, have developed their beliefs from those early dabblings in esotericism that began among the members of the Straight Track Club. These ley hunters still look back to Watkins as the founder of their discipline, but in doing so they tend to interpret his discovery more mysteriously than he seems ever to have viewed it himself. His son and biographer was part of this process in 1972, when he described his father's insight as having had 'all the marks of an ancestral memory'.[35] But the chief populariser of the view that Alfred Watkins was a psychic without realising it was the visionary and prolific New Age author John Michell, who in 1969 argued that 'in his own mind Watkins knew that leys were something other than roads of commerce', describing the Herefordshire businessman as having had 'a transcendental perception' that allowed him to enter 'a magic world'.[36]

After Alfred Watkins, Michell has been perhaps the most influential figure in the history of ley hunting in Great Britain. That history seemed to hibernate for about twenty years in the mid-twentieth century. The Straight Track Club was officially wound up in 1948. By then, many of its key members had died and others had been 'converted' to orthodox archaeology, while the war in 1939 had effectively put an end to much of the club's activity.[37] For the next two decades, there was little interest in Britain's ley lines. In 1962, a rather odd little pamphlet titled 'Skyways and Landmarks' was published, in which its author Tony Wedd suggested that UFOs followed the course of ley lines, either because, like wartime bombers, they were navigating by ancient landmarks, or because (like the migrating birds observed by members of the Straight Track Club) they were detecting lines of magnetic current.[38] This spawned a minor two-year flurry of interest that saw the founding of the *Ley Hunter* magazine and the Ley Hunters' Club by a group of 'ufologists'.[39] It was not until 1969, though – that psychedelic year that gave birth to the Woodstock festival, *Abbey Road*, and man's first steps on the moon – that ley hunting had its real renaissance, with the publication of the first full-length post-Watkins book devoted to ley lines, Michell's now classic volume *The View Over Atlantis*.

John Michell reconceptualised ley lines. Instantly solving the age-old problem of their mad trajectory across bogs and mountains, he argued that the lines were not in fact tracks. Their aligned monuments and geographical features were not there to direct travellers. Instead, the lines of barrows, standing stones, churches and hilltops revealed the course of 'energy streams', as if they were great stone and earth pylons supporting invisible wires across the countryside. The energy that they carried Michell called 'terrestrial magnetism', explaining that although it was little understood any longer, 'all the evidence from the remote past points to the conclusion that the earth's magnetism was not only known to men some thousands of years ago but provided them with a source of energy and inspiration to which their whole civilization was tuned'.[40]

For Michell, moreover, the ley markers were not there simply to indicate where energy lines existed; their role was more active than that. 'The most remarkable feature of the whole system is that the paths of [. . .] magnetic flow are not naturally straight; they spiral and undulate like surface rivers or currents of air; yet the currents that follow pre-historic alignments are as direct and regular below ground as are the leys on the surface,' he wrote, concluding that 'the present pattern of the earth currents in Britain must be of artificial origin'. So for Michell, our ancient ancestors had lined up earthworks and monuments with natural features in the same way as the nineteenth century's engineers had planned canal routes through locks, tunnels and aqueducts as a means of sending coal around the country. Except that the fuel carried by the leys was an invisible power; one that, harnessed into the right channels, could provide the 'spiritual irrigation of the countryside'.[41]

John Michell's theories drew on two earlier thinkers as well as Alfred Watkins. The first was the controversial Austrian psychoanalyst Wilhelm Reich, who in the 1940s claimed to have discovered a new form of energy – a life force he called 'orgone'. For Michell, this was identical to his 'terrestrial magnetism'. Indeed, he claimed that the 'orgone accumulators' that Reich invented – artificial chambers intended to intensify orgone and so create heightened states of consciousness – were identical in design to the prehistoric chambered tombs found on so many ley lines.[42]

The second important influence on Michell was Alexander Thom, a retired professor of engineering from the University of Oxford. Two years before *The View Over Atlantis* appeared, Thom's own book, *Megalithic Sites in Britain*, had been published, arguing on the basis of his precise measurements of megalithic monuments that the early inhabitants of prehistoric Britain had not been grunting savages but had possessed a detailed knowledge of mathematics, geometry, surveying and astronomy.[43] His theories opened the door to new views of prehistoric man that required him to have had an understanding equal, if not superior, to that of his modern descendants – the sort of intellect necessary to align huge monuments over scores (and even hundreds) of miles, or to discover, control and then direct an invisible source of energy.

After some initial resistance, Thom's book eventually found its way on to the bookshelves of the archaeological establishment.[44] Michell's beliefs, however, were either stoically ignored or else ridiculed by orthodox archaeologists. Like Watkins before him, Michell met with the objection that his ley markers were a hotchpotch of sites built at different periods: Victorian churches linked to stone circles; medieval castles to Roman burials. Furthermore, in the most sustained attack on his ideas, Williamson and Bellamy's *Ley Lines in Question*, even some of Michell's 'prehistoric' mark stones are rubbished, dismissed as modern gateposts, random boulders, or rubbing posts for horses, sheep and cattle.[45]

Williamson and Bellamy roundly mocked the idea of a force that 'can be conducted by ponds and hilltops, that runs to a mark stone the size of a football because it is on an alignment and avoids similar stones that are not, and is totally undetectable by scientific instruments'.[46] However, Michell's book was a huge popular success.

By 1973, it was on to its third edition. And over the next decade it gave birth to a whole progeny of ley hunting guides that nearly all looked to it as their founding document. Even today, many books on ley lines are haunted by the presence of the late John Michell: if they do not have a foreword or introduction by the great ley hunter himself, then they quote lavishly from the evocative words of the man who has been described, even by his detractors, as 'the great prose poet of ley lines'.[47]

In the 1970s, ley lines seeped into the national consciousness. They appeared frequently in articles written for the underground press;[48] they manifested mysteriously in the lyrics of rock songs;[49] and young adventurers discovered their arcane powers in children's fantasy novels and on television.[50] As with Watkins, Michell's book had fortuitously appeared at just the right moment in time. By 1969, Britain's suburbs were spreading like an oil slick across the green fields that had once separated its cities. New towns were springing up like crops of bright orange mushrooms. The first supermarkets were dazzling consumers with their neon-lit corridors of tins. And the country's motorway system was reaching its grey tentacles the length and breadth of Britain. 'As everyone knows,' Michell reminded his readers, 'the earth is slowly dying of poison.'[51] Ley lines held out a vision of an older, gentler way of life. A whole generation that was seeking alternatives to consumerism, urban expansion and modern technology looked out across the fields and moors of the British countryside . . . and saw long, soothing straight lines.

The lost golden age that Michell and his ley hunters looked back to was not always the prehistoric world in which, they believed, ley lines had been created. It was also sometimes the simple, pre-war world of Alfred Watkins. According to Michell, this had been when 'for the last time the landscape could be seen in its old form', before 'the imposition of meaningless, secular patterns'.[52] Both *The View Over Atlantis* and a whole school of ley hunting books that followed it in the 1970s were illustrated with Watkins' black and white photographs of horses, carts, and the sort of small, hedged meadows that had been gradually lost since the 1920s, as part of the growth of large-scale agribusiness. The anti-urban, anti-modern appeal of ley lines in the 1970s appears most strikingly, perhaps, in the introduction to Paul Devereux's 1979 guide *The Ley-Hunter's Companion*, which laments how 'great cities sprawl into the countryside, forming conurbations that breed their own consciousness; automobiles hurtle along motorways that are merely urban arms stretching across the landscape between towns [. . .] Even those who live and work in the countryside have their rural sensibility subtly eroded by radio, television and other media. [. . .] There are no mental city limits.'[53]

Devereux assured his readers, though, that 'beneath this complex of urban consciousness the landscape still broods, the elemental cycles of the planet still function'. Ley hunting in the 1970s and 1980s, then, was not only a means of rediscovering the past; it was also a way for alienated city-dwellers to reconnect with nature. Devereux's book promised to open doors to 'a remote time when people's lives were closely in step with elemental and spiritual realities, when the landscape, the heavens and the human mind were understood as one deeply interdependent whole'.[54] And ley hunting was not just about nostalgia for this time. Michell had imagined that the 'life essence' he'd discovered could be the medium through which the earth's 'restoration will one day, inevitably, be brought about'.[55] By the late 1970s, when Devereux was writing hopefully of the 'salvaging of such prehistoric science' in the wake of a decade of oil crises and miners' strikes, his readers must have been enticed by the possibility that 'earth energy' might prove a clean, free, inexhaustible alternative to the flickering, uncertain power supplied by the National Grid.

During the seventies and early eighties in Britain, Paul Devereux was one of a small group of ley hunters who became interested in seeking academic legitimation for their view of the past. One way in which they attempted to gain this was by using statistics, and the newly available tool of computer modelling, to demonstrate that the likelihood of finding five, six or even seven aligned sites to make up a ley line was well beyond any arrangement that might occur if the giant hand of chance were to randomly scatter hand-fuls of megaliths, castles and churches across the countryside.[56] Suddenly mathematicians were drafted into the ranks of ley hunters – and some of these, like Chris Hutton-Squire and Pat Gadsby (who in 1976 computer-modelled ley lines running through mega-liths at Land's End), were at least tentatively converted by the evidence they found.[57]

Another way of seeking academic approval was by engaging in debate with archaeologists. With a few exceptions, though, the advances of ley hunters in that direction met with tight-lipped silence. Having tried and failed to 'find any meaningful public discussion about leys (either for or against) on the part of archae-ologists', Paul Devereux, for one, concluded that 'the fundamental desire not to believe' among professional archaeologists 'would prove a psychological study in itself'.[58] An academic study of ley lines was finally published in 1983 by two Cambridge graduates. However, after their 200-page book had announced as its grand conclusion that ley hunting was 'a pathetic alternative to conven-tional archaeology', ley hunters tended to retreat back within the protective lines of their own discipline.[59]

In truth, ley hunting was never really an 'alternative' to archae-ology – in Britain's intellectual ether it has always hovered closer to faith than to science. John Michell himself was never too worried about validation of his ideas by 'experts'. 'The ley system,' he mused, 'may actually be invisible to those whose previous know-ledge tells them that it cannot exist.'[60] Today, similarly, for the London ley hunter Christopher Street, leys 'may be compared to the hidden knowledge of a secret tradition. Freely available to those in the know. Totally invisible to those who aren't.'[61]

Archaeologists may shake their collective beards over all this. How can you argue, remonstrated Williamson and Bellamy, against authors who freely admit they have no hard evidence to back up their ideas?[62] But where archaeologists can spend whole heated conferences arguing with venom over small but salient points of interpretation, ley hunting is a broad church of beliefs where contradictions are tolerated, intuition is accepted as valid, and widely varying interpretations of the same basic facts happily co-exist. The Society of Ley Hunters, for instance, 'has not prepared a single formal definition of a ley and recognises that there are many opinions'; it embraces both those who view ley lines as the ancient tracks rediscovered by Alfred Watkins, and those who consider them to be the conduits for John Michell's earth energy.[63] And most ley hunters are happy to disagree on questions such as whether ley markers create or just reveal the direction of energy lines, without feeling the need to settle on one absolute explanation.

Likewise, they cheerfully differ in their opinions of what the ley map of Britain looks like, and where its most important lines are. 'Contrary to popular belief,' the website of the Society of Ley Hunters announces, 'there is no national register of ley lines. They are there to be found by you; should you want to.'[64] The society, along with the Network of Ley Hunters, is one of the country's main ley hunting organisations. It regularly receives queries from members of the public wanting information about the whereabouts of ley lines in their own area. 'One of our recent requests, for instance,' its secretary Eric Sargeant told me, 'was from somebody in Bristol, wanting to know whether the city's Hall of Jehovah's Witnesses was built near a ley line.'[65] The response to such requests most often comes in the form of advice about possible sites in the vicinity that could be investigated on the ground to search for an alignment. At the essence of ley hunting is independent exploration and discovery. Consequently, for the hundreds of ley hunters in Britain, there are hundreds of different, individualised maps of the country. One man's empty moor has another man's eight-mile-long expressway crossing it.

Having said this, just as information was exchanged in Watkins' day, many of today's ley hunters share their routes at the biannual conferences of the ley hunting societies, in the pages of their journals, and on the internet. 'The web has made a phenomenal difference to ley hunters,' says Eric Sargeant, who himself has painstakingly plotted leys contributed by dozens of members of the Society of Ley Hunters on to the online maps of Google Earth. And while most ley hunters primarily spend time discovering and mapping ley lines in their local area, there is also a shared core of classic routes that criss-cross Britain and that have become pilgrimage sites for the nation's ley hunters.

Some of the most famous of these are the original ley lines mapped by Alfred Watkins. There is, says Eric Sargeant, often 'an element of pilgrimage' involved today when ley hunters retrace the uncertain footsteps with which Watkins followed his very first ley. This ran for 27 kilometres through the Herefordshire country-side from the Iron Age hill fort of Croft Ambrey to the Roman camp of Stretton Grandison.[66] Watkins then went on, in *Early British Trackways*, to publish details of another seven routes all likewise around Hereford. That city, then, is the Canterbury or perhaps the Iona on the ley hunter's map of Britain – the place where their history (as opposed to their prehistory) began. Appropriately, it is also in Hereford library that ley hunting's earliest chronicles are held, in the form of the original portfolios of Watkins' Straight Track Club.

In his later full-length books on ley hunting, Watkins identified a score of lines intersecting the Welsh valley of Radnor, a group of 15 ley lines that interlaced Berkshire (with Windsor Castle at their centre), a small mesh of ancient tracks on Salisbury Plain, and numerous lines in the countryside around Cambridge. These areas have all since become classic ley hunting Meccas. But Watkins also found individual ley lines elsewhere in Britain, and many of these were later revisited in the guidebooks of other ley authors 'as a tribute' to him.[67] They include a famous ley running from the Devil's Arrows in Yorkshire; the two lines believed to dissect Oxford like a huge invisible crucifix; and the four ancient tracks thought to link churches, palaces and hilltops in London.[68] These often-visited and well-loved routes have become the Pennine Way, the Lyke Wake Walk, and the West Highland Way of the ley hunter's Britain.

The best-known ley line in Britain, however – the MI of the ley hunter's map – is also the country's longest. It is thought to link Land's End with Lowestoft over more than 350 miles, like a great diagonal sash sitting around the widest point of England's hips. The roll of sites along its length reads like an antiquary's to-do list: Glastonbury, Avebury, the abbey of Bury St Edmunds, Cornwall's Cheesewring (though it also passes through some of the least likely towns to sit on a sacred alignment: Luton, Letchworth, Trowbridge). However, it is the line of hilltop churches dedicated to St Michael (most famously St Michael's Mount, off the coast of Cornwall) that gives the ley its name.

The Michael Line, as it is now known, was first identified by John Michell in the late 1960s. Michell believed that in the prehistoric past, 'a continuous sacred track' had run along the full length of the ley – Britain's equivalent of the Camino Francés that leads Christian pilgrims to Santiago di Compostela in Spain. A few stretches of it could still be identified: 'At Glastonbury [. . .] the Pilgrim's Path still runs right along the ridge of the Tor, and at Avebury the line exactly coincides for over three miles with what is now the main road to Devizes.'[69] Michell linked the ley to the 'dragon lines' believed in Chinese feng shui to carry a magnetic-like energy across the earth, pointing out that not only had Michael been a dragon-slaying saint, but also that the ley strings together several hilltop shrines to other famous dragon killers, such as St George and St Margaret.

The Michael Line's fame and popularity among ley hunters was later cemented by a full-length book devoted to the route. On 1 February 1987, the dowser and blacksmith Hamish Miller and the author and photographer Paul Broadhurst set out from St Michael's Mount in their native Cornwall on a quest to track the full length of the ley across southern England. Over the course of the next two years, the pair of pilgrims followed its route to tiny chapels 'buzzing with an almost audible static', to stone circles that seemed to be 'nerve centres' where the line intersected with an intricate knot of smaller leys, and to holy wells just a stone's throw from busy roads or 'soulless bungalows' yet so atmospheric that 'no one would be in the least surprised to catch a glimpse [. . .] of the faery folk'.[70] After much scrutinising of maps, deliberation in muddy fields, crossing and recrossing of the M5, and retracing of weary footsteps, they came to the conclusion that the Michael Line was not a straight and narrow Watkinsinian alignment, but rather one of the arterial and naturally serpentine paths of energy that straight ley lines are often believed to feed off. Prehistoric peoples had lit beacons along its length at May Day and other festivals,[71] while Victorian chapels and Georgian follies had been deliberately built in its path, either 'by intellect or intuition'.[72] Today it continues to suffuse the sites along its length with an indefinable energy.

Miller and Broadhurst also concluded that the Michael Line has a twin – the Mary Line – which meanders alongside it like a partner in some mysterious and ancient dance. And they later traced the course of another great ley line, which they named the Apollo-Athena Line. This international ley is believed to begin at Skellig St Michael (a small island off the south-west coast of Ireland), to traverse Cornwall, and then to head across France, Italy and Greece on its way to Turkey. There is one other huge, motorway-like ley line believed to stretch across Britain. In 1974, Guy Raglan Philips identified a line extending from Lee-on-Solent (near Portsmouth) up the spine of Britain through Winchester, Birmingham, Carlisle and Inverness to Inverhope on the north coast of the Scottish Highlands. He named it the Belinus Line after a legendary road-building British king who, according to the medieval monk Geoffrey of Monmouth, 'summoned workmen from all over the island and ordered them to construct a road of stones and mortar which would bisect the island longitudinally from the Cornish Sea to the shore of Caithness and should lead in a straight line to each of the cities en-route'.[73]

Whether or not the Belinus Line really runs along the course of King Belinus' road (if that ever existed), both it and Britain's other long-distance leys are now routes recognised and travelled by ley hunting communities. The Michael Line, in particular, has been walked by hundreds of dedicated ley hunters since details of its route were first published in 1969 – most of those visitors British, but others travelling from Europe, America or the southern hemisphere to experience the ley's energies.[74] While many walkers attempt only short sections of the route, others approach its 350-mile length in the spirit of a true pilgrimage. Indeed, in 2010, the not-for-profit organisation 'Mary Michael Pilgrims Way' began work to establish a recognised pilgrim's route along the line, erecting a series of wooden waymarks, organising group tours, and publishing their first pilot guidebook (covering the 140-mile stretch from Brentor on Dartmoor to Glastonbury) a year later.[75]

If short ley lines have come in for criticism from sceptics, though, Britain's long-distance leys have been even more vehemently attacked. In *Ley Lines in Question*, Tom Williamson and Liz Bellamy bewailed the lack of prehistoric markers located on the Belinus Line, lamenting Guy Raglan Philips' reliance on 'roads and paths [. . .] groves of trees, a few farms [. . .] a line of gorse bushes' and scoffing at his description of the line as a 'highly visible' feature of Britain's landscape.[76] They also pointed out that John Michell's Michael Line manages to take in none of Wiltshire's twenty churches dedicated to St Michael on its course through that county, concluding that 'we cannot help feeling that John Michell has been singularly unfortunate in his choice of line, for random chance could no doubt connect a more convincing series of ancient points than those traversed by his hapless long-distance dragon'.[77]

Ley hunters have responded by arguing that Britain's long-distance routes should not be understood as simple alignments of sites, but rather as 'geomantic corridors' a couple of miles wide, which thus embrace all of those pesky churches and other monuments that seem to just miss being precisely positioned on the ley. The Michael Line, Paul Devereux and Ian Thomson concluded in 1979, is 'a corridor of significance rather than a narrow line of sites. [. . .] We offer the term geomantic corridors to describe such lines. There need be no problem encountered in accepting that the phenomenon of ancient geomantic alignments probably falls into different categories. Roads, for example, have many forms, from dirt tracks to motorways.'[78]

Besides his controversial Michael Line, John Michell also identified two ley lines that joined together churches and earthworks on the Bedfordshire–Hertfordshire border; one that linked megaliths like stone beads in the countryside outside Aberdeen; and another that ran finger-like down the spine of the Isle of Man. The best known of his shorter ley lines, though, are the two that he found linking standing stones on the Land's End peninsula in Cornwall, which have appeared in many later guidebooks, and were twice chosen to test the statistical proof for ley lines in the 1970s and 1980s.[79]

The south-west of England – the counties of Cornwall, Devon and Somerset – is today one of the most popular centres for ley hunting, because of the quantity of prehistoric remains there, and because the open tracts of Dartmoor, Exmoor, and Bodmin Moor allow leys to be followed with few of the access problems encountered in other areas. Dartmoor, in particular, with its avenues of standing stones that, like starting stalls, seem designed to send the ley hunter galloping off in straight trajectories, has long been popular as a place to find your own leys. Also, perhaps, the military presence on the moor means that the area has never been short of men who know how to handle a compass. In Watkins' day, a Major F. C. Tyler (who later took over leadership of the Straight Track Club) traced 'some 20 alignments' on the moor, the details of which were published in the *Devon and Cornwall Notes and Queries* for October 1925.[80] Today, retired colonel John Christian has spent many hours there (often on horseback, like a latter-day Watkins) plotting uncharted sections of the Mary ley, which was previously known only to enter the moor at the church-topped rock of Brent Tor and then leave near St Mary's church in Dunsford.

Other areas that have seen recent attempts to 'fill in the gaps' on Britain's ley map include Lincolnshire, Leicestershire, Nottinghamshire and County Durham – all counties more or less ignored by Alfred Watkins.[81] Indeed, Durham has the curious distinction of being probably the only county in which Watkins found no ley lines at all during the course of writing his three books on the subject.[82]

Not all modern-day ley hunting takes place on windswept moors or through ancient oak woods, though. Christopher Street is co-ordinating a project to map the ley lines that intersect with the busy streets of Britain's capital. In 2010, his first book on this subject, *London's Leylines*, was published, which added 12 new lines to the four that Alfred Watkins had found in London. He is now collating information from contributors, Watkins-like, to publish a second guide to metropolitan ley lines. Street's energy paths run parallel to Fleet Street, cut through Piccadilly Circus, brush invisibly past the shops of Covent Garden, and conclude dramatically on the summits of Primrose Hill and Parliament Hill. The most important ley line in London, he argues – the Pall Mall of its ley map – runs in the direction of the midsummer sunrise from St George's Hill in Weybridge to a crossroads in Chigwell Row, Essex. Along its route it links together Westminster Abbey, St Paul's Cathedral, and the site of the 'king stone' in Kingston upon Thames – all sites 'associated with the coronation of Britain's monarchs'.[83] For Street, this is 'an extremely important axis of power relative to the entire country' that 'somehow esoterically aligns the king with the sun to empower his rule over the land'.[84]

Reading Christopher Street's descriptions of lost stone circles, hidden holy wells, empty churches filled with angelic singing, and prehistoric mounds disguised as traffic islands, it is difficult not to feel that he lives in an alternative London, a hidden capital, incandescent with magic, that somehow exists between the lines of the city most Londoners recognise. Ley hunting seems to have the power to transfigure even mundane landscapes. The most striking example of this is probably found in the work that Anthony Poulton-Smith has done tracing the vestiges of ancient pathways across the flat face of the Midlands. Whether weaving through shoppers in the centre of Tamworth, or gingerly treading along a narrow strip of greenery sandwiched between the M1 and the A4532, the author of the unfailingly optimistic guidebook *Ley Lines Across the Midlands* forever manages to see beyond the litter and the crowds, to ignore the roar of articulated lorries, and to dream of days when wolves and boar roamed, and when hardy traders strode from stone circle to hilltop carrying precious loads of salt.[85]

Poulton-Smith's latter-day quest was not without its tests and impediments, however – its own 'Slough of Despond' and 'Doubting Castle' to be negotiated by the hopeful ley pilgrim. Trying to walk the route of a 50-kilometre ley line from Malvern to Brailes, for instance, he realised that modern roads, railways and private land meant that he needed to cover 'at least seventy miles (and probably more)'. Attempting to follow another ley line between the towns of Syston and Asfordby, he discovered that he would need to ford the River Wreake five times in the space of just two kilometres to stay on the right track. And tracing a 30-kilometre alignment between Bardon Hill (an extinct volcano) and Burrough Hill (a hill fort) in Leicestershire, he found that in order to avoid trespassing, he was forced to walk parallel to the route he'd intended to take, making only periodic excursions to the ley line itself to search for ancient sites, succeeding in finding 'almost none' despite his hopes of it being 'a promising region'.[86]

One particular problem faced by ley hunters like Anthony Poulton-Smith is that the markers that define the lines can be tricky, deceptive guides. Churches that seem to stand on ancient sites may turn out, after further research, to have been destroyed in the nineteenth century and rebuilt further down the village. Mark stones may have been moved from one field to act as a handy gatepost in another. And avenues of trees aligned with distant hills may simply be the result of eighteenth-century tastes in gardening. For this reason, the ley hunter's map of Britain is forever shifting uncomfortably around, changing every time a fresh ruler and a critical eye reveal a small wiggle, or a new local history takes two centuries off the date of a building. This quality provides the source of much humorous anecdote in John Timpson's millennial account of his alternative tour around Britain, *Timpson's Leylines: A Layman Tracking the Leys*. From searching in vain for significant notches in hills, to mistaking an ornamental folly for an ancient saint's well, the author ends up in no end of scrapes in his quest to follow in the footsteps of Alfred Watkins. More seriously, though, the difficulty also caused one of Britain's most respected ley researchers, Paul Devereux, to substantially rewrite his 1979 guidebook *The Ley-Hunter's Companion*, rejecting many of its ley lines in his 1994 work *The New Ley Hunter's Guide*, and later to dramatically renounce his whole theory of ley lines across Britain's landscape.

Ley hunting, it seems, is an activity that has always been beset by all kinds of difficulties, and which has demanded true perseverance and commitment from its adherents. Alfred Watkins records that, while trying to prove the alignment of New Radnor Castle with Old Radnor Church using photography, he was obliged to climb a steep bank four times carrying a heavy camera, 'incidentally breaking a bone in my foot on a wet slope'.[87] And many of the surviving photographs of the Straight Track Club show both men and women scrambling with difficulty up banks and through dense undergrowth in pursuit of the next ley marker.

It is not just difficult terrain, inconvenient fences and uncertain ancient markers that confront the modern-day ley hunter in pursuit of their quest, though. If you are interested in leys, Christopher Street warns, 'first and foremost you should be equipped with a thick skin [. . .] because the subject is an easy target for the cynical,

the sceptical and the shallow opportunistic comedian. Some of
your oldest friends will assume that somewhere down the ley line
you have lost your marbles.'[88] For this reason, much ley hunting
(particularly in urban areas) takes place while most of us are still
dozing under duvets, attracting inquisitive looks only from street
sweepers, bamboozled partygoers heading homewards, and sleep-
less mothers pushing wailing infants.

Those ley hunters who perhaps attract the most quizzical stares
in the early hours are the dowsers. On a search for leys in the centre
of Torbay, Alan Neal describes receiving 'inquisitive looks from
several elderly people [. . .] as I crossed over the ley and my rods
mysteriously swung together in unison'.[89] While many ley hunters
still stick to Alfred Watkins' carefully outlined method of identifying
ley lines on an OS map using a straight edge and glass-headed pins,
others today (especially those searching not for ancient tracks but
for energy lines) search using dowsing rods.

Alan Neal suggests that the easiest way to begin dowsing for ley
lines is to 'practise on a line whose existence has been established
using the conventional map method'.[90] Holding out a pair of
L-shaped metal rods (classically made from bent coat-hangers) so
that they point straight ahead, the dowser needs to approach the
right general area, he advises, with a clear idea in their mind of
the ley line for which they are searching. As they draw nearer to
it, their rods will cross; if they overshoot, the rods will point back-
wards.[91] In this way, the route of a ley line can be traced without
any need for a map or even mark points. Indeed, dowsers like the
retired army colonel John Christian describe almost bumping
straight into great megaliths by accident as they intently follow
their rods along the course of a ley.

Grahame Gardner, the president of the British Society of
Dowsers, has been dowsing for ley lines in this way around the
Glasgow area since his teens, though he tells me that most dowsers
today tend to be over 40 – it's a preoccupation that people often
come to later in life. For him, leys can be dowsed as easily as

underground water courses, though Watkins' straight lines between monuments are just one feature on Gardner's ley map of the country. The view of Britain shared by Grahame Gardner, John Christian and most other ley hunting dowsers is one in which the country is intricately enmeshed by a complicated cat's-cradle of energy currents. 'It's like the road system,' John Christian muses. 'The energy lines are all different strengths and they bifurcate and bifurcate. The big ones, which people sometimes describe as leys, are like motorways or autobahns. But then intersecting with those you also have your A roads, all the way down to single-track roads, and finally sheep tracks.' So if someone says they have a ley running through their garden, he explains, what they really have most of the time is just an energy line – the ley hunter's equivalent of a side street or country lane.

The majority of the energy lines on the dowser's map of Britain are neither straight nor static. Some wind like snakes. Others vibrate to and fro like guitar strings. There are, Grahame Gardner says, 'more categories than we have words for'. It is up to the individual dowser, moving quietly though this complicated landscape, to make sense of it all: to intuit which are the most powerful and important currents crossing the countryside.

Intuition is an important skill in the world of ley hunting, whether divining for earth energy or simply searching for ancient traders' routes. Ley hunters spend much of their time simply sensing the atmosphere of a location – communing with its energy to effect changes in either the place or themselves. Alan Neal, on his journey around the south-west's ley lines, experienced 'quite spontaneous feelings of inner peace and well-being' at seemingly mundane crossroads, and intimations of historical importance along the course of minor farm tracks.[92]

On their quest along the Michael Line, Hamish Miller and Paul Broadhurst spent much time connecting with the spirit of various churches and sites – from the 'intense black atmosphere' of Lydford church, to the 'primitive and pure' ambience at St Germoe's church in Cornwall, to the 'mystic potency' and 'unnerving but uplifting air' of Glastonbury.[93] And, following in Miller and Broadhurst's footsteps in 2009, the Australian ley hunter François Capmeil spent long hours basking in the atmosphere of St Michael's Mount, growing to recognise the 'definite change' in himself created by the site. 'Spending time on the lines has an effect on consciousness,' he mused. 'So the pilgrims of the Middle Ages had it right, they did not come back home the same as when they left.'[94]

St Michael's Mount is a particularly potent site for Britain's ley hunters, as it is the point at which the Michael and Mary lines intersect with that international ley highway, the Apollo and Athena line. It is, perhaps, the St Pancras of the ley hunter's Britain. For many ley hunters, the points where leys cross are more important than the lines themselves – their energy, it is believed, is concentrated at those sites, like the confluence of two rivers in full spate, or the streams of shoppers on Oxford Street and Regent Street meeting in a seething maelstrom at Oxford Circus. It is believed that in prehistoric times, stone circles were constructed to mark these invisible crossroads, and that millennia later, in the Middle Ages and even as late as the nineteenth century, churches were built on the sites to channel their energy for spiritual purposes.[95]

Whether or not medieval masons deliberately built churches at points where leys cross, there are certainly people today who choose important locations based on beliefs about where lines intersect. In 1990, the astrologer Michael Cainer bought a house in the village of Oulston, 12 miles north of York, at least partly because he believed that two lines crossed in its paddock. 'Where they cross, power is generated,' he said. 'I stand here and always come away re-energised. It's the psychic equivalent of a large Scotch.'[96] And the new town of Milton Keynes is believed to have been planned so that ley lines intersect in its centre, 'to draw in positive energy into the city'.[97]

Besides St Michael's Mount, the most important crossing points on the ley map of the country include Glastonbury, Stonehenge, Avebury and Canterbury – all sites to which ley hunters flock in droves. On a day-to-day basis, however, most ley hunters resort to favoured neighbouring sites. 'All ley pilgrims seem to have their own local sites that are most important to them,' Christopher Street says. 'Mine are St Mary's hilltop in East Barnet and Camelot Moat in Trent Park.'[98] This is particularly true of dowsers. 'A lot of dowsers,' Grahame Gardner says, 'are more comfortable on home turf. Some dowsers are better on chalk, others on clay, for instance. When you're comfortable in the landscape, it's easier to get an energetic connection with it.'[99]

Connecting with the land is an important part of the appeal of ley hunting, the Devon dowser John Christian says. He also gets 'a deep satisfaction' from tracing their course. 'A feeling of well-being. And a confidence that there is more out there than twenty-first-century humans understand.'[100] For many ley hunters, a sense of rediscovering forgotten knowledge, or of simply connecting with the past, is also central to the pursuit's charm. Hamish Miller and Paul Broadhurst felt 'drawn back to an earlier time' at Boscawen-Un stone circle.[101] And at Avebury, they were 'drawn back to a world where this stupendous temple had been deliberately planned and constructed'.[102] Even for a vehemently rational ley hunter of the traditional Watkins school like Anthony Poulton-Smith, the idea of following in the footsteps of prehistoric traders is 'a quite moving experience'.[103]

Importantly, the past that Britain's ley hunters seek is a past to which everyone has free access. For those who believe in ley theory, it is possible to connect with something very ancient just by sitting in a clearing in the woods, or by climbing a hill. Unlike the academic discipline of archaeology, there is no need for training or plastic gloves, there are few restrictions on access to most sites, and it's not necessary to have waded through countless academic papers before offering an interpretation of any discoveries.

One of the most alluring and exciting aspects of ley hunting is the prospect of stumbling upon undiscovered ancient remains simply by following the course of a line. Sometimes this seems to happen quite literally. While ley hunting in a field just north of Walwick in the 1970s, Paul Devereux recounts how he found '[. . .] a stone or pillar about six feet high on the line of the ley, which came as a surprise to us as we almost bumped into it in the course of following the ley's bearing. Nothing is marked on the maps we used, and the O.S. does not have a record of the stone. [. . .] It seems to have been marked on only one map, in 1925, when it was shown with two others some distance apart. It may only be a rubbing post, but this fact, together with its position dead on the ley, suggests an earlier feature.'[104] More recently, John Christian followed his dowsing rods along the Michael Line on Dartmoor to find what is now known as the Belstone Ring Cross – an Anglo-Saxon carved granite marker – propped up against the outer wall of Belstone church. 'I must have walked past it hundreds of times without noticing it, but there it was. Somebody at some time had placed it there, right in the path of the Michael Line. The dowsing rods led me straight to it. I sat down on a grave and said, "Bloody hell",' he laughs. In a small country that has been searched, surveyed and sieved for centuries, few other opportunities like this present themselves to the enterprising and intuitive individual longing to make their own archaeological discoveries.

Predictably, many professional archaeologists have serious doubts about the ley hunters' techniques. Tom Williamson and Liz Bellamy protest that 'as far as we know, no ley hunter has ever discovered a genuine prehistoric site by this method'.[105] However, John Christian's Belstone Ring Cross has been acknowledged as an important historical find by the Dartmoor National Park Authority, as the earliest evidence of Christianity in that village. In 2005 it was mounted on a plinth inside the church and given its own information board.

Whether or not ley hunters discover unsuspected prehistoric sites, what they do unarguably encounter along the course of ley lines is the rich heritage, the unrivalled quirkiness and the varied beauty of the British countryside. And besides becoming a dab hand with a map and compass, one of the undeniably positive side effects of ley hunting is that it invariably leads enthusiasts into the study of Britain's history, its archaeology, its place names and its folklore – and from there to a richer and more colourful relationship with the country. This is as true for the doubtful sceptic tentatively following their first ley as it is for the most committed dowser of energy lines. When the journalist John Timpson set out on a millennial quest to see what he could discover by following Britain's ley lines, his aim was neither to prove nor disprove ley theory, but simply 'to discover where these lines might take me, and what I might find along their route'.[106] What he found were griffins, dragons and green men crouching in medieval churches, villages where spectral gypsies and highwaymen wailed, and the footprints of the giants who once strode across Britain's moors.

The ley hunter's Britain is a land of continual surprise and discovery. Almost a century ago, Alfred Watkins promised his disciples that 'the great multiplicity of leys in a small area will surprise and perplex you', but the seemingly endless growth and infilling of Britain's ley map means that any individual armed with a compass, a map and a pair of good shoes can still become a latter-day Columbus, embarked on 'a new voyage of discovery' without needing to leave their own back yard.[107] Numerous hidden centres and countless unknown ways await the ley hunter, secreted in the country's seemingly bland suburbs and invisibly overlaying its well-trodden city centres. And our rural spaces are often as crowded with these busily intersecting routes as our metropolises. For John Christian, 'In my mind's eye, I can see power points littered all over the countryside.'

Back in the pubs of Hereford, few of the rugby fans crowded in front of the giant television screens would see any point in trekking along an invisible, uncertain and arguably improbable route joining the city's cathedral with three medieval churches and an

Iron Age camp perched on a distant hilltop. For many ley hunters, though, the ley map of Britain reveals the country's international status far more meaningfully than do the successes of its sporting teams. For Grahame Gardner, John Christian and others, the Michael and Apollo lines are two of just twelve great global energy currents that form a grid around the earth. And the fact that these important long-distance energy lines pass through our island proves 'what an important place England was' in prehistoric times. 'The whole country,' John Christian explains, 'was important globally.'[108] Indeed, Britain's leys may not only connect the country internationally; for some ley hunters, like Christopher Street, they also have a vertical dimension to them, 'with connections off-planet and to the heart of the Earth's inner core'.[109]

Golden wires connecting Britain to the cosmos. The veins of the living earth. Nature's version of the National Grid. Or simply ancient trackways. There seem to be as many different ways of thinking about the ley map of Britain as there are versions of the map itself, or varieties of ley hunters following its mysterious alignments – from map-reading surveyors searching for salt routes to dreadlocked drummers playing as a way of 're-energising' the lines. What perhaps unites all ley hunters, though, is a deep sense of responsibility for the country in which we live, and a vision of interconnectedness that cuts through Britain's regional, national, social and religious boundaries. Whether or not we believe that ley lines exist, the ley map of Britain with its countless surprising connections should perhaps be a model for the ways in which we think about our own links with the past and the future, and the complex, unsuspected relationships that we have with neighbours both nearby and also across the length and breadth of the country.

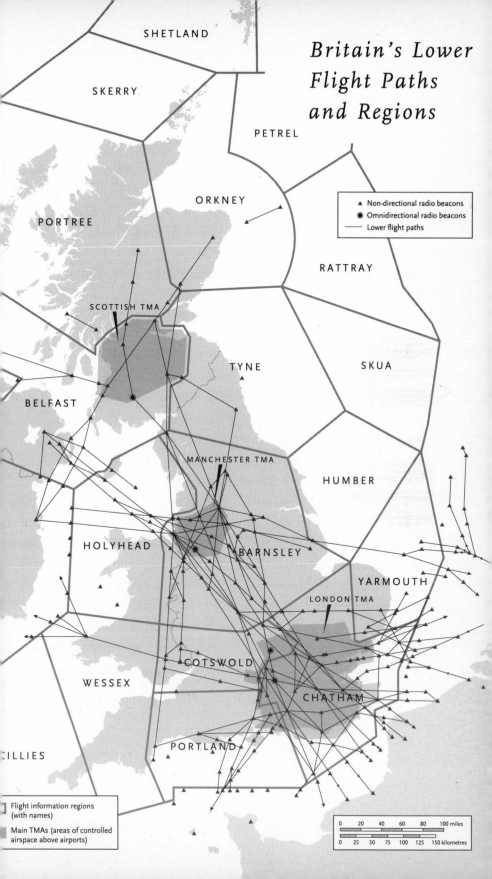

Britain's Lower Flight Paths and Regions

SHETLAND

SKERRY

PETREL

ORKNEY

PORTREE

RATTRAY

▲ Non-directional radio beacons
◉ Omnidirectional radio beacons
— Lower flight paths

SCOTTISH TMA

TYNE

SKUA

BELFAST

MANCHESTER TMA

HUMBER

HOLYHEAD

BARNSLEY

YARMOUTH

LONDON TMA

COTSWOLD

CHATHAM

WESSEX

PORTLAND

CILLIES

Flight information regions
(with names)

Main TMAs (areas of controlled
airspace above airports)

0   20   40   60   80   100 miles
0   25   50   75   100   125   150 kilometres

Britain's Lower Airspace

SHETLAND
Sumburgh

ORKNEY

LEWIS

SCOTLAND

Aberdeen

North Sea

Edinburgh
Glasgow

Prestwick

Belfast City

Belfast

Newcastle

Durham
Tees Valley

Isle of Man

Leeds
Bradford

Doncaster Sheffield

Manchester

ENGLAND

East Midlands

Norwich

WALES

Birmingham

Luton

Brize Norton

Stansted

Heathrow — City

Cardiff

Bristol

Gatwick

Bournemouth

Southampton

GUERNSEY

JERSEY

Blocks of controlled airspace (above an airport) from the ground up to a set height in the lower airspace. Aircraft can only enter if the pilot is using instrument to navigate — no access for most light aircraft.

Blocks of controlled airspace (above an airport) from the ground up to a set height in the lower airspace. Aircraft in which the pilot is navigating visually (most light aircraft) can enter, but only if given clearance.

Corridors of controlled airspace around flight paths, between set altitude. Only pilots using instruments to navigate can enter — no access for most light aircraft.

Corridors of controlled airspace around flight paths, between set altitude. Pilots flying visually (most light aircraft) can enter, but only if given clearance.

0   20   40   60   80   100 m
0   25   50   75   100 125 150 kilom

5

Highways in the Air:
The Map of Britain's Skies

It must have been one of those splendid Scottish mornings when the clear sky looks as if it has been freshly scoured. The year was around AD 832. On the plains of lowland Scotland, not far from St Andrews, the Pictish king Angus MacFergus and his troops gathered to defend their lands against the invading Northumbrian king Athelstan. As the battle began, King Angus no doubt reassured his nervous troops that a vision of Christ's disciple Andrew had appeared to him the night before, promising victory. But it was only when that saint's emblem – the diagonal cross on which he had been crucified – actually appeared in the heavens overhead that the Picts gained heart. They overcame Athelstan and gained a momentous victory. As for the vast white saltire set against the blue sky, it not only changed the course of history, it was also adopted as the banner of the grateful Picts, and then in 843 became the flag of all Scotland.[1]

In the days of King Angus, the skies above Britain were God's blank pages on which to emblazon signs and omens. For centuries they were an empty stage across which comets might streak, presaging war or pestilence, or in which new stars might blaze, announcing royal births. Their only tenants were the flocks of birds that came and went with the seasons; their only features the ever-changing clouds by day, and the shifting constellations of stars and planets at night. For the Romantic poets, the skies were more lonesome than the emptiest fells. Percy Shelley thought them infinite, lonely and silent. Wordsworth famously wandered 'lonely as a cloud'. For Victorian authors like Dickens, musing over social inequities and religious doubt, the heavens were 'forlorn and empty'. And even in the early twentieth century, D. H. Lawrence huddled his Derbyshire pit villages under an 'empty sky'.

Standing in the fields outside St Andrews today, though, Angus MacFergus might puzzle over any number of strange celestial hiero- glyphs – white lines and crosses appearing regularly against the blue like the brushstrokes of a giant watercolourist. Britain's skies are now rarely empty. They have always seemed to be a vast mirror image of the countryside below – on a summer's day, their candy- floss islands of white cumulus clouds seem to perfectly echo the jelly-mould outlines of broadleaf copses dotted across fields. Just as those woods and meadows have been sliced and severed by highways and motorways, though, so too the vast field of blue above is now etched with a complicated spider's web of routes linking our major airports with each other.

Britain's airways may be all but invisible to most of us – seen only in glimpses, while vapour trails hover momentarily along their paths like ghostly footprints – but like the motorway system on the country's surface, they are in fact vast thoroughfares that often carry heavy traffic. Known to pilots as Air Traffic Service Routes, or more simply 'ATS routes', they are usually 10 miles wide – broad enough to allow for any drift of planes left or right when trying to follow a straight bearing in difficult weather conditions. Like motorways, again, it is possible for multiple vehicles to share the same route, but instead of travelling alongside each other, planes are stacked vertically, each on a different 'flight level', usually with 1,000 feet between aircraft. The lowest planes travelling between Britain's airports on these millefeuille freeways are typically 5,000 to 7,000 feet above our heads (expressed respectively as flight levels 50 and 70). The highest are 24,500 feet up – at flight level 245.[2]

The airspace dissected by Britain's flight paths is organised laterally into different zones; 24,500 feet up, where the sky is starkly blue and oxygen begins to be restricted, is the point at which 'lower airspace' turns into 'upper airspace'. Here too there is a labyrinth of flight paths above Britain – the 'upper ATS routes', or 'upper airways'. But rather than connecting Britain's airports to each other, these aerial highways (which can be accessed from the lower ATS routes) are long-distance international thoroughfares, linking us with the shrinking world beyond our shores.

The upper airways are predominantly the preserve of commercial airlines conveying dozing, chatting, film-watching passengers around the globe. However, like Salisbury Plain or Dartmoor, our country's upper airspace is also a region where Britain's civilian and military worlds overlap, with another set of aerial routes carrying rather different traffic. Flight Lieutenant Michael Lyddon, or 'Geordie', is part of the team of military air traffic controllers responsible for the use of Britain's TACAN (Tactical Aid to Navigation) routes. He explains that this network of corridors, which stretches the length and breadth of the country alongside the upper airways, is used for military air transport and for RAF flight training.

But military flying also takes place outside of the TACAN routes. 'A high proportion of military aircraft within the Upper Air are fast-jet aircraft,' Geordie says. 'Due to the nature of their operation, they would be unnecessarily restricted by having to fly along specified UAR or TACAN routes.'[3] It is the job of military air traffic controllers like himself to ensure that these high-speed off-piste air users are safely directed across and between the wide official routes of Britain's upper air. This often requires careful negotiation and co-ordination with civilian air traffic controllers, he says, particularly at night and weekends, when commercial airlines are now sometimes allowed to cut corners through the upper atmosphere, leaving the airways briefly to fly direct from point A to B as a means of conserving fuel.

The possibility of leaving the airways if weather or traffic conditions make this necessary (or if air traffic control allows it as a means of saving fuel) is one huge difference between Britain's motorway system and its aeronautical map. How many car drivers must have gazed wistfully at the fields lying between a gridlocked M5 and the slip road they need to take? In many other ways, though, Britain's airways closely mirror its highways.

Like most of our roads – the A30 to Truro, the B939 to St Andrews – Britain's airways are coded with short strings of numbers and letters. Those in the upper airspace always begin with the letter U. The military TACAN routes all begin with T. In the lower airspace, names are usually made up of one letter followed by one, two or three numbers. These routes are all marked on the aeronautical equivalent of the *AA Book of the Road* – the Airac charts, produced by the Civil Aviation Authority.

On a bright summer's day at Breighton airfield in Yorkshire, with planes taking off every few minutes behind us, I pore over the Airac charts with flying instructor Mickey Kaye and commercial pilot Peter Gill. The outline of Britain on the maps is of course familiar, and by looking at this and at the seething convergence of routes in certain areas, it's fairly easy for an amateur to guess at where the major cities must be located. But the Airac charts – unlike some aeronautical charts – don't bother setting their aerial world against what exists on the ground. 'If I'm flying at 24,000 feet, I'm not interested in what colour the grass is,' laughs Peter, a man with 38,000 hours' flying under his boiler suit. 'When you can see Blackpool illuminations while you're flying over Guernsey, you don't need much detail.'[4]

We focus on looking at the charts of the lower airways – at the complicated maze of corridors below 24,500 feet that, like our roads and railways, is there to connect Britain's cities. It includes some tiny routes, adrift and independent from the main system, like the short airway (N580) that ties the southern Hebrides to the Scottish mainland. Other airways straddle great swathes of the country

– the M1 and M6 motorways of the air. The P600 cuts north-east to south-west across southern Scotland, like half of King Angus's great saltire, on its way from Aberdeen to Dublin. Angus MacFergus might have caught a glimpse of its trail had he lived 1,200 years later than he did.

Further south is the L10, which travels north-west to south-east on its way from Belfast to Dover, passing over the Wirral, Birmingham and London on its way. The N615 bisects the country the other way, cutting north–south from Glasgow to the Sussex coast by Worthing, passing over Manchester and – again – Birmingham en route. Much like Britain's road system, on the map of Britain's airways there is a dense spinal cord of air routes that runs through England's Midlands to fan out in the cortex of its south-east corner.[5]

As well as the main ATC routes, the Airac charts also show 'conditional routes' that are available only at weekends, or that can be used tactically at the discretion of the country's air traffic controllers, like opening the hard shoulder to relieve gridlock on a motorway at rush hour.[6] Mickey Kaye explains that the Airac charts are used by all commercial pilots planning journeys along the airways, who are required to submit a 'flight plan' outlining their intended route and timings before departure. It's a strictly controlled business. Once it has been approved, the flight plan must be followed exactly, with the pilot passing waymarks at fixed altitudes and at precisely the right times. This ensures that air traffic controllers are able to keep aircraft separated by a safe distance of at least five nautical miles, and a thousand feet laterally, at all times. Adherence to the flight plan is carefully monitored using radar – Britain's airways are a place of constant surveillance.[7]

The map of Britain's airways also has as many administrative and legislative boundaries as does the country's surface. Mickey tells me that the airways form part of what is known as 'controlled airspace' – the most strictly policed sectors of our heavens. Within that category, they are also usually classified as either 'Class A' or

'Class D'. In Class A airspace, absolutely all aircraft will have been separated by air traffic control, will be monitored using radar, and will be in radio contact with air traffic controllers at all times – so in practice, the only planes there are usually commercial airliners. Class D airspace is slightly less restrictive; although most traffic will be travelling in accordance with a flight plan, it is also possible for private flights that have not submitted a plan to join the airway, provided that they request permission to do so ten minutes before joining it, and that they remain in radio contact with air traffic control at all times.

Besides the corridor-like airways, Britain's controlled airspace also includes great blocks of sky immediately above most of the country's airports, as well as the space higher up where aircraft begin manoeuvring for their descent. In areas like London, where there are several airports clustered together and numerous airways converging, there might additionally be a wider and higher swathe of controlled airspace shared by a number of neighbouring airports. 'If you could see the controlled airspace above Heathrow, for instance,' Mickey says, 'it would look like an upside-down wedding cake, with the biggest tier at the top – that's the terminal manoeuvring area shared by all the London airports. Then below that there'd be a smaller tier, which is the terminal control area. And then finally there'd be the control zone around the airport itself – the smallest tier going right down to the ground. Britain is unusual,' he adds, 'in having controlled airspace that goes right down to the ground. In most countries that isn't the case.'

Britain's airspace is also parcelled up geographically into 32 regions – a little like the counties and districts that determine who cleans our streets and who charges us for water. One of the functions of these 'flight information regions' is to determine what local altimeter settings pilots must adopt, to ensure that all flights in that particular district really are flying at the correct altitudes. The names of many of the regions simply echo the towns or counties beneath them – Humber, Barnsley, Cotswold, Holyhead.

Others, though, are named more poetically. In the far north of the British Isles, flanking the Shetland Isles, are Puffin, Petrel and Marlin, while the feathery Skua flutters offshore beyond Northumbria.[8]

Every day, around 7,000 flights leave their wispy trails along Britain's airways – or more than two million per year.[9] It is dizzying to think about the rate at which this never-sleeping, strictly controlled web has been spun out of truly empty space. It is only a little over 200 years ago that the ether above our country was quite literally virgin territory. Despite being one of the most technologically competitive and keenly colonising nations of the late eighteenth century, Britain was relatively late in penetrating its heavens. Almost a year elapsed between the flight of the world's earliest manned hot air balloon, in Paris on 21 November 1783, and the first tentative exploration of Britain's skies.[10] In that time, more than a score of other balloons (both hot air and hydrogen-powered) navigated the skies of France and Spain, but it was not until late in 1784 that the first tiny steps were taken towards traversing – and eventually mapping – Britain's airspace.

Those steps, like the tottering of any infant, were initially faltering and hesitant. On 10 August of that year, a large crowd watched, crestfallen, as a balloon tried and failed to take off from Chelsea bowling green. Among the spectators was the rather satisfied Italian Vincenzo Lunardi, who had laid a 20-guinea wager that the flight would fail.[11] Eight days later, he announced to the press that he would be making his own attempt to enter Britain's airspace, and on 15 September (in a balloon tactfully decorated with a vast Union Jack, to mitigate suspicions about an Italian aloft in British skies), he took off from a stage on London's Royal Artillery Ground in the company of a pigeon, a lapdog, and a cat (who was later thrown out of the basket, to the outrage of some commentators).[12]

There was only a small crowd at the Royal Artillery Ground that day to watch the historic first entry into Britain's skies. The press put this down to disillusionment after the failure at Chelsea, and to public suspicion that the event was merely an elaborate hoax. Once the balloon was aloft above London, though, it didn't take long for every roof and church spire to be filled with limpet-like spectators, getting as close as possible to the route of the 'beautiful stupendous globe'.[13] In total, that first trip above Britain lasted for about three and a quarter hours – time enough for its pilot to polish off twelve glasses of wine. The balloon skimmed above St Paul's, continued on a westerly course until it was close to the border of Bedfordshire, and then proceeded north past Horsey and Hatfield in Hertfordshire before landing at the village of Colliers End near Ware – which should be remembered as a sort of Pilgrim's Point of British air travel. Although he alighted just 26 miles from his launch site as the crow flies, Lunardi estimated that he had travelled between 50 and 60 miles.

The reactions of those on the ground below the balloon's course seem to have ranged from astonishment to terror. In London itself, a Mrs Saunders of Goodge Street reportedly died from the shock of seeing a flag and an oar drop from the sky as Lunardi passed over Islington. Near Horsey, the Italian hailed 'wondering spectators' through a trumpet as the balloon briefly neared the ground. It was at the village of Northaw in Hertfordshire that the cat landed in a cottage garden (without any apparent injury). And as the balloon finally prepared to descend, the inhabitants of Colliers End showed 'great marks of terror'.[14]

Just one month after Lunardi's pioneer flight from London, one of his greatest ballooning rivals, the French 'aeronaut' Jean-Pierre Blanchard, successfully took off from Chelsea, travelling 73 miles – first to Sunbury in Surrey and then on to Romsey in Hampshire.[15] And in the following decades, residents of the greater London area must gradually have got a little more used to the idea of travel above their heads, as other flights took off from the capital. By the 1820s, with the discovery that coal gas could be cheaply used to fill balloons, London became the ballooning capital of Britain, with a number of operators offering short sightseeing trips above the city for the wealthy and curious, as well as launches from parks for the entertainment of the masses.[16]

Balloons also began to take off from elsewhere in the country. There is some controversy surrounding the next location to have staked its place on the aerial map of Britain. A Mr Sadier claimed to have taken to the air in Oxford on 4 October 1784 – a date that would make it the country's second flight after Lunardi's. However, since he was apparently 'neither seen in his ascent or descent', most of his contemporaries rudely dismissed the claim.[17] Forgetting Sadier, the next recorded locations at which Britain's ether was entered were Norwich, on 22 July 1785, and Chester, on 8 September of that year. The Norwich flight was an attempt to raise funds for the newly opened Norwich and Norfolk Hospital, using a balloon borrowed for the occasion from London. Under the inexpert guidance of a Major John Money (who had only been up in a balloon once before), it rose into the air in front of a distinguished and enthusiastic crowd of spectators and was then carried north-westwards towards Lincolnshire. Disaster struck as it gained height, however, for it was blown back across Norwich by a higher-altitude air current before continuing south-eastwards towards the Norfolk coast. It was last spotted over Lowestoft, before crashing 20 miles into the North Sea. Amazingly, after five hours in the water, Money was rescued and was hailed as a hero.[18]

The proximity of the sea was also a keen concern for the Chester flight. Its pilot, a Mr James Baldwin, who was a native of the city, had tied an array of bladders to the outside of the balloon's basket in case he too should end up in the drink. And as he set off, these precautions seemed wise, as the wind initially carried him directly towards the coast. He was more fortunate, however, and after a few tense moments he entered a higher airstream and proceeded towards the Mersey. He descended briefly into a field at Kingsley, just south of Frodham, and finally landed at Rixton Moss on the outskirts of Warrington in Lancashire.[19]

The evident difficulty of controlling the course of the earliest balloon flights meant that there was little sense in the eighteenth century that Britain's air would ever be a truly useful medium for transport.[20] A few dreamers came up with theoretical uses for balloons beyond public entertainment. Benjamin Franklin imagined that 5,000 hydrogen balloons could be used to lift an army of 10,000 men across the English Channel to stage an invasion.[21] And in the mid-nineteenth century, after longer-distance balloon flights had carried their pilots as far as Belgium and Germany, Tennyson dreamt that one day the air might be used to facilitate international commerce.[22] But from the 1840s, once the railways had begun to spread their dependable iron across the country, for most people the future of transport lay on and under the ground, and flying through the air was simply a rich man's means of adventure.[23]

In the 1860s, however, one practical application for balloons was discovered. In February of that year, the British Association began negotiations to acquire a balloon in order to explore the upper levels of Britain's air – what we now commonly know as 'the stratosphere', the region higher than six miles or 32,000 feet from the surface.[24] Leading the project was James Glaisher, head of the Department of Magnetism and Meteorology at the Royal Observatory in Greenwich, and the first man to have produced national daily weather reports in Britain. This was a means of furthering his research into weather conditions. At the time, virtually nothing was known about the country's upper airspace. Did it, for instance, get hotter or colder as one travelled higher? Was there breathable air up there?[25]

Wolverhampton was chosen as the site for Glaisher's experiments, both because it was geographically close to the centre of Britain, and because it had a dependable and helpful gasworks that could provide fuel for the flights. The project did not begin well. The first balloon acquired by the Association was an elderly vessel that only managed to rise a quarter of a mile, dragging its pilots through treetops before it crash-landed seven miles from the gasworks launch site.[26] The second balloon, made for the project by the experienced aeronaut Henry Tracy Coxwell, split when it was filled for take-off, causing the crowd of spectators to beat a hasty retreat.[27] Finally, though, on 17 July 1862, Glaisher and Coxwell took off successfully, reaching a little over 20,000 feet in just two hours. Glaisher recorded both the atmospheric conditions and those of his own body, observing that his pulse increased and his hands and lips became dark bluish, and that the sky was deep blue in colour.[28] The local press reported with satisfaction that on their descent to the village of Langham (between Peterborough and Leicester), the pair had drunk the health of the Queen, the British Association and the town of Wolverhampton.[29]

Glaisher's most celebrated high-altitude flight, though, took place on 5 September of that year. On that record-breaking ascent, he and Coxwell passed through the 20,000-foot barrier, where breathing becomes harder, after just 40 minutes. After 54 minutes (still assiduously taking regular measurements of the temperature, atmospheric pressure and so on), they were at 29,000 feet. What their maximum height was remains a mystery, because at that point Glaisher was unconscious from asphyxia and Coxwell (himself light-headed, frostbitten, and experiencing loss of muscle power) was desperately fighting to lower the balloon. It must have been between 35,000 and 36,000 feet, but it was certainly higher than six miles. The pair eventually descended from the stratosphere to land near Ludlow in Shropshire, whereupon they had to walk seven or eight miles to the nearest village, Cold Weston.[30]

After that September flight, Glaisher and Coxwell reluctantly became national heroes, and more and more of their flights took place in the south of England – at Windsor Great Park or the Crystal Palace – where the launches could be watched by large crowds.[31] They never again flew as high as on that September day in the Midlands, so Wolverhampton should forever retain a brown sign on the aeronautical map of Britain, as the point from which the British stratosphere was first breached.

In the decade after Glaisher's meteorological flights, another practical use began to be made of balloons – as military observation platforms. In 1878, the Royal Engineers began constructing a balloon that made its first ascent on 23 August of that year over

Woolwich. The balloon was deemed a useful new tool, and two years later a military School of Ballooning opened and began launching regular training and test flights over the town. The school later moved to Chatham in Kent, to Aldershot in Hampshire, and then finally – in the winter of 1904 – to the eastern edge of Farnborough Common in Hampshire, in quest of larger and larger premises as aerial surveillance began to be used more and more successfully in overseas combat.[32]

'The Balloon Factory', as it was now known, did not only send balloons up into the air over England's rolling North Downs, however. By 1905 it was also experimenting with man-lifting kites, following the controversial appointment of the military's first 'kiting instructor' – a charismatic native American who had first moved to Britain as a performer, demonstrating sharp-shooting, bareback stunts, and kite spectacles at shows around the country.[33] Samuel Cody first began offering his services to the military in 1901, but it was only after he had broken the kiting altitude record (sending one soaring 14,000 feet into the heavens above Worthing in 1902), and also crossed the English Channel in a canoe towed by a kite, that the War Office decided to takes kites seriously. Army personnel could soon be seen aloft at Farnborough, strapped below kites that were then released from their cables so the pilot could glide back to the ground.[34]

These flights were not, in fact, the first attempts at gliding in Britain. The earliest experiment had taken place in 1853, when the eccentric aristocrat George Cayley had persuaded his coachman to sit in a boat-like contraption with a wing above it that he then rolled down a steep hillside at Brompton Dale near Scarborough. That contraption had stayed only briefly aloft before it crashed to the ground.[35] Cody's gliding kites were far more successful. They were, however, unpowered, and therefore entirely at the mercy of wind conditions.

The Balloon Factory experimented with various forms of powered flight in the first decade of the twentieth century. After

Count Zeppelin had flown his first airship in Germany in 1900, they worked on constructing an airship for Britain.[36] *Nulli Secundus* – 'Second to None' – launched successfully from Farnborough on 5 October 1907. It flew 40 miles north-east to London, passing over Bagshot, Staines and Chiswick en route. Cody sounded a klaxon as they approached the capital, in order to warn anybody who might have failed to notice the enormous inflated vessel hovering 800 feet above their heads. It literally stopped the traffic in central London for half an hour, flying over the Crystal Palace, Hyde Park, Buckingham Palace, Whitehall and St Paul's. Unable because of high winds to fly back to Farnborough, however, the airship was forced to land in London, and when it was later disassembled to travel home ingloriously by road, it was badly damaged and returned as a cripple that would never fly again.[37]

Other British military airships followed, but none was particularly successful. However, the sad fate of *Nulli Secundus* presented an opportunity to Sam Cody. He began experimenting with fixing its discarded engine to one of his gliding kites, in an attempt to emulate two bicycle makers who, on 17 December 1903, had taken briefly to the air from the sand dunes of the small North Carolina island of Kitty Hawk, on board the world's first working aeroplane.

The first flight of Wilbur and Orville Wright's 'powered flyer' had lasted just 12 seconds and had covered a distance shorter than the wingspan of a Boeing 747 plane.[38] But by the end of their first day of test flights they had managed a whole minute in the air and a distance of 850 feet, and by the start of 1905 – a year later – they were able to fly for almost three miles.[39] News of the flight does not seem to have caused much immediate excitement among the general public in Britain – perhaps not surprising, since it was reported in the press as the take-off of a 'balloonless airship', and many assumed that it was simply a hoax.[40] By the time the Wrights were performing daily flying demonstrations in France, however, an urgent race was under way in Britain to produce the first British aeroplane.

Technically, it was at Blair Atholl in Scotland that an aeroplane first lurched into Britain's skies. The flight, piloted by Lieutenant John Dunne, was the culmination of a military-funded project that had been carried out in strict secrecy. The plane itself travelled to Scotland from Farnborough accompanied by plain-clothes military engineers to avoid attracting unwanted attention, and the residents of the Highland village were instructed to stay indoors with their curtains closed for the duration of the test. They did not miss much. The flight was sadly brief – the aircraft stayed aloft for just forty feet before it crashed into a dry-stone wall. Since Britain's recently established Royal Aero Club had decreed that in order to qualify as the country's first aeroplane flight, any trip would have to cover at least a quarter of a mile, the competition to accomplish this continued.[41]

Several other short flights punctured Britain's airspace like the tiniest of embroidery stitches throughout the summer of 1908 – at Blair Atholl, at Farnborough, and at Brooklands Aerodrome, near Weybridge in Surrey. By 16 October, though, Samuel Cody had made enough short take-offs and had done enough subsequent tinkering to feel sufficiently confident to invite the press to Farnborough Common to observe the take-off of his 'Army Aeroplane No. 1'.

Cody's machine had been built on a tight budget. It was constructed of hickory and bamboo, its engine had come from a motorboat, and its cloth-covered wings had been stiffened with tapioca. But a Union Jack fluttered optimistically behind it as it set off down a short hillside. The plane leaped into the air, rose to a height of between 20 and 30 feet, and flew north-west over a small clump of trees. As Cody tried to avoid a second, taller spinney, though, one wing tip touched the ground and the machine crashed, damaging its engine, wheels and left wing. Cody himself was more fortunate, suffering only a cut to his forehead. More importantly, he was victorious. His aeroplane had been airborne for less than a minute, but it had flown 424 metres, making Farnborough Common the first place in Britain to have officially seen the take-off of a heavier-than-air flying machine.[42]

Farnborough will always be regarded with reverence by Britain's aviation enthusiasts. Like Drake's Plymouth, it was not only the launch site of a single momentous voyage, but also the point of departure to a whole new world. The tree to which Cody allegedly tied 'Army Aeroplane No. 1' while testing its pulling power died in 1940, but like a saintly relic it was filled with resin and mounted in concrete to preserve it indefinitely.[43] The common and its airfield are not only revered as the site of Britain's first aeroplane flight, however. It was there in 1912 that the Royal Flying Corps (later to become the RAF) was formed. In 1924 it became the first place in the country to send high-altitude aircraft into the heavens. And it was at Farnborough in 1925 that Britain's first helicopter flights were made.[44] The site's life as the capital of British research flying ended on 25 March 1994, after nearly 90 years, but Farnborough still looks heavenward. A private flying club and an aviation company both operate there today. And as well as the visitor centre commemorating Farnborough's pivotal role in British aviation history, the common is home to a poignant but proud family of memorials to the men who first flew and died there – including Cody, who died on 7 August 1913 when a waterplane that he was flying crashed on the north-western corner of the airfield.[45]

Although Cody is remembered today as a great pioneer of British aviation, the initial reactions of the press to his first successful flight were not particularly positive. Most reporters focused more on reporting the crash than the flight itself – the *Manchester Guardian*, for instance, was typical in titling its report 'Army Aeroplane Wrecked'.

The British government was also unimpressed. The following April, it decreed that all aeroplane experiments by His Majesty's Balloon Factory were to be terminated 'as there was no future for them'. The short-sighted decision was overturned after just a year, and in the meantime, privately funded aviation projects continued.

That year saw the opening of the Aeronautical Syndicate – the first private aeroplane manufacturing company in Britain – which was given permission to test its machines above Salisbury Plain. Another company quickly followed, this time test-flying on the Isle of Sheppey, just off the north coast of Kent.[46] The following year, Britain's first flying schools opened, using Farnborough Common and Salisbury Plain as their airfields.[47]

By the end of 1911, most regions of England and lowland Scotland had seen aeroplanes. Throughout 1910, the British and Colonial Aeroplane Company had staged spectacular flying displays in the heart of Bristol.[48] April of that year had seen a 185-mile London-to-Manchester race for aeroplanes. But the real christening of Britain's skies took place in July 1911, when the Circuit of Britain Air Race, sponsored by the *Daily Mail*, took place – a 1,010-mile time trial around the country, starting at the Brooklands airfield in Surrey and taking in Hendon, Harrogate, Newcastle, Edinburgh, Stirling, Glasgow, Carlisle, Manchester, Bristol, Exeter, Larkhill and Brighton, like a long ribbon tied around the country.[49]

Forty thousand spectators turned out to see the 21 competitors set off from Brooklands on 22 July. At Hendon, their descent was watched by 'a crowd entirely without precedent'.[50] At Manchester, later that week, a hopeful audience scanned the skies for more than four hours hoping to catch a glimpse of the English contender James Valentine (who had in fact been forced to make an emergency landing at Widnes). And even by 28 July – by which time the winner, André Beaumont, had already received his cheque for £10,000 – a crowd of 10,000 turned out in Stirling to cheer on the straggler Samuel Cody, who was still only halfway around the circuit.[51] For many of these crowds – especially those living far away from any airfield – it would have been the first time they had seen aeroplanes aloft in Britain's skies.

Just three years later, such entertaining spectacles came to an end, when all civil aviation was prohibited at the outbreak of the Great War.[52] Military flying took over on the sites of Britain's existing airfields. Initially the pilots taking off from these sites worked simply as aerial chauffeurs, carrying senior officers over enemy territory. Gradually, their role in reconnaissance increased. And by the summer of 1915, fighter pilots with machine guns mounted on their planes were taking to the air.[53] As aviation assumed an increasing importance to the war effort, many of Britain's pre-war battlefields were enlarged as part of a sudden and urgent race to train fresh legions of pilots and to increase the country's store of military planes (by 1917, Britain and France were producing 30,000 aircraft a year).[54] Trees were cleared from Farnborough Common to allow for a massive increase in the use of that airfield, and more and more flights climbed into the air above Salisbury Plain.[55]

If they had seen planes flying before, it was nonetheless during the war that the residents of Britain became acutely aware that the skies above their heads were a medium connecting them to mainland Europe. Bombs first began to be dropped from the air on to Britain in 1915, using Zeppelin airships, and from the summer of 1917 they were being deployed using faster, agile planes.[56] In total, over a hundred such raids were made on the country.[57] In response, new British airfields were built around the outskirts of cities, to protect likely targets more immediately from the air. The skies of London were by far the busiest aerial location in Britain at this time, with planes regularly swarming overhead like an Egyptian plague of locusts, but south coast ports like Dover and Folkestone also saw regular aerial visitations, as did the towns of England's Midlands.[58]

London's skies were never again going to be the still and silent abode of stars and angels. One of the new airfields to be created as a defence measure during the war was Beddington Aerodrome near Croydon in south London. After the war, it was one of the many military airfields that were transferred to civilian use. Amalgamated with a neighbouring test-flying ground, Waddon Aerodrome, it reopened its doors on 29 March 1920 as Croydon Airport. Today, planes no longer take to the air from Croydon, but the borough has a strong claim to be remembered as the site of

Britain's first proper airport – though Blackpool International Airport, which was a public airfield from 1909 until 1911 and then reopened as an airport in 1932, also claims that honour.[59]

Certainly, Croydon had the first purpose-built airport terminal in the world, which was opened in 1928. It also quickly became the centre of the British Empire's airmail network, with sacks of letters rising daily into its skies like clouds, to be carried as far afield as India, South Africa and Australia. And it was one of the first places in Britain to see regular international flights taking off, flying to Paris, Amsterdam and Rotterdam from 1920, and to Berlin from 1923.[60]

In fact, the world's very first scheduled international flights began flying out of Folkestone in 1916, carrying just two passengers at a time to the Belgian city of Ghent. Two other regular routes from London to Paris followed in 1919 – one from RAF Hendon and the other from Hounslow Heath. Over the next two decades, other passenger airports were opened around Britain, including Manchester in 1926, Bristol in 1930, and Aberdeen in 1934. When war erupted again, many of these were temporarily closed and others were converted into RAF fighter stations to defend London, ports such as Plymouth, Cardiff and Glasgow, and industrial centres like Birmingham from aerial bombing. After Britain had increased its own use of aerial bombardment in 1942, some existing airfields also became bases for Britain's bombers. The sight of vast formations of these taking to the air, like flocks of ill-omened birds with characteristic calls, became familiar in East Anglia and Yorkshire, in particular, in the last years of the war.

Croydon Airport was among those that served as a fighter station throughout the war, and it played a front-line role in the Battle of Britain, which raged above London in September and October 1940 – the first major battle in history to have been fought entirely in the air.[61] Before the war was even over, though, doubts were being aired about the small airport's ability to remain the nucleus of British airspace. And once Armistice Day had been celebrated, and it was clear that in the future aircraft were going to become bigger and more numerous, those discussions intensified. In 1946, the first flight (to Buenos Aires) took off from a new London airport – Heathrow. By 1952, it had been announced that Croydon would close. And the last scheduled plane flew out of Britain's first airport on 30 September 1959.[62]

Since 1946, Heathrow Airport has remained at the heart of Britain's aeronautical map. The country now has more than 50 airports offering scheduled flights, spread across the country from the Shetland Isles to the Scillies, and ranging from tiny sites like Barra Airport in the Outer Hebrides (at which just one airline operates short hops through Britain's skies) to multi-terminal monsters like London Gatwick and Manchester (the country's busiest airports after Heathrow), which launch planes to locations across the country and around the world. No other British airport, though, is anything like as busy as Heathrow, a bubbling cauldron of activity that sees more than 1,200 planes arrive or leave every day. It is the umbilical cord that links our little island to the rest of the world. Known as the country's 'hub' airport, it connects us to more than 75 global locations not served by any other British airport.[63]

In the decades since Heathrow opened, air traffic above our country has increased exponentially. In 1949, 18,000 flights a year were crossing Britain's airspace. By 1985, that figure had increased to a million. It now stands at more than twice that figure.[64] Such a high volume of traffic requires vigilant monitoring and careful policing. The organisation responsible for overseeing the movement of controlled air traffic when it is 'en route', travelling along the airways between Britain's airports, is NATS – the National Air Traffic Control Service, founded in 1962. NATS has two main bases for its operations: at Prestwick, in Ayrshire, and at Swanwick, on the Hampshire coast near Southampton. Between them, these two nerve centres divide up control of Britain's skies. Prestwick's radars monitor all airways in Scotland and Northern Ireland, as well as many of those around Manchester, while Swanwick's controllers oversee the majority of flight paths in England and Wales, including those in the busy London area.

Flying along Britain's airways today, there is no real possibility of becoming lost. It is a far cry from the early days of flying, when pilots had to rely on 'dead reckoning' to estimate their position – using a combination of their speed, direction, and the wind resistance. Inevitably, they often wandered off course, particularly in poor weather conditions or at night.[65] The problem of navigation in aeroplanes was first tackled in America in 1926, when gas- and electric-powered beacons were installed across the country – a network of land-locked lighthouses that allowed the night-flying airmail planes to see their way. These illuminated guides were useless in fog or low cloud, however, so in the mid-1930s, a system of radio beacons was set up, whose Morse code signals could be detected in planes using a simple receiver.[66]

The first radio beacons were installed in Britain during the late wartime period.[67] These non-directional beacons (known as NDBs) emitted just one signal, like the beam of a single torch. They only allowed pilots to gauge whether they were flying to the left, to the right, or straight along the course of the beam, judging by whether they could hear a steady tone (meaning that they were on the beam) or a broken one. However, the NDBs did make it possible for pilots to plot a journey from beacon to beacon, and so navigate a fairly accurate course. And it was the spider's web of long straight beams from these beacons that first created the network of fixed airways that appeared in the late 1940s and still exists in our skies today.[68]

NDB still beam their signals into Britain's skies. In the 1950s, though, many of them were replaced by variable omnidirectional ranging beacons (known as VORs). Like tiny suns, these emit a radial pattern of 360 radio beams into the air, making it possible for pilots to plot their position with far more accuracy.[69] Today, NDBs and VORs continue to be used by some pilots, alongside

GPS technology and radar. Hundreds of NDBs and more than 50 VORs are spaced throughout the British Isles – the inconspicuous NDBs looking like any other aerial; the VORs like huge metal sunflower heads facing up to the sky. The beacons are one of the few terrestrial features marked on the Airac charts. Their names range from abbreviations of familiar place names – Bel in Belfast, Gow in Glasgow, Ranok in the Scottish Highlands – to the oddly cosy-sounding Sandy, Cathy and Monty, and the downright odd Guntu, Sapco and Vapid.[70] They continue to be the main road signs guiding the way through Britain's heavens, and the main waymarks used for flight planning by air traffic control.

Air traffic control at Britain's airports began long before the creation of centralised 'en route' control. For the first decades of the twentieth century, however, its methods were extremely basic, with controllers simply waving a green or red flag at airfields to indicate whether it was safe for a plane to take off. By 1920, when Croydon Airport opened, the flag had been replaced by a light gun firing a red or green flare.[71] It was not until the 1930s that air traffic control towers equipped with radio began to be built. Pilots radioed their position to the tower and controllers there updated a map showing the position of all planes in the area, radioing pilots if there was any risk of a collision.[72] This was the main means of controlling air traffic in Britain until 1950, when (following technical advances made during the war) the first civil radar equipment was installed at the new Heathrow Airport to assist with take-offs and landings.[73]

Today, air traffic control at airports is divided in two. Aerodrome controllers sit like eagles at the top of the air traffic control towers that are now a familiar sight at every airport. Using both their eyrie-like vantage point and radar, they deal with aircraft during taxiing, take-off and landing. Once planes are in the air, however, they move over to the jurisdiction of the approach controllers, who are also based in the control tower but are often behind tinted glass as they work entirely through radar. Approach controllers are responsible for moving planes from the airways down through the inverted wedding cake of the airport's controlled airspace (and vice versa). Often this involves directing arriving pilots to a 'stack' – a fixed area in which several aircraft circle whilst waiting to land, one above the other like a stack of plates balanced on a juggler's arm. Most of Britain's airports have several of these invisible multidimensional roundabouts in the skies above them (though in some cases this may mean twenty miles away). Heathrow has four – Bovingdon, Lambourne, Ockham and Biggin, named after the places beneath them – which have been in the same locations since the 1960s.

Approach controllers are also often responsible for guiding departing planes along steeply climbing three-kilometre-wide corridors known as noise preferential routes, which must be followed exactly for the first 4,000 feet of the plane's ascent. These invisible stairways above many of our airports, particularly in London, were set up by the Department for Transport in the 1960s to avoid low flying over built-up areas – though housing development since then means that some communities today do live close to the routes used by planes to fly up into Britain's network of airways.[74]

Many of us live directly beneath airways without really being aware of the thoroughfare above our heads. In the 1940s and 1950s, an immensely long international airway known as 'Amber One' passed directly over the Lake District National Park on its way around the world. Today, sections of it still exist between Britain and Japan; the stretch above the Lakeland fells is now known as N615.[75] In its decades of inscribing white lines above Cumbria's heather-tufted summits, though, that airway has disturbed few walkers or residents, simply because of its height. Planes travelling along N615 are usually at an altitude of between 14,500 and 19,500 feet, so even from the mountaintops they are still a good distance off.[76] As planes begin to descend through the huge inverted ziggurats above our airports, however, communities are often all too aware that they are living beneath busy, controlled airspace.

Ninety-one thousand people live beneath the approach and landing paths at Manchester Airport. But that figure is dwarfed by the 181,000 who are affected by the noise of planes landing and taking off at Heathrow.[77] Generally, planes prepare to land at Heathrow from the east and take off to the west – though this switches around if the wind is blowing from the east (in Britain it is usually westerly), since aircraft need to take off into the wind.[78] This means that the London boroughs of Hounslow and Richmond upon Thames, due east of Heathrow's runways, are the areas worst affected by the sound of landing aircraft – in Hounslow's school playgrounds, teachers have found that they are inaudible for 25 out of every 90 seconds.[79] Windsor, on the other hand, is directly in the path of departing planes. However, as John Stewart of the Heathrow Association for the Control of Aircraft Noise (or HACAN) explains, the steep ascent that planes are legally required to make these days means that take-offs produce less noise than long, low landings. Indeed, landing noise can affect homes well away from airports. 'It can be a problem twenty miles away,' John says. 'People move into those areas and don't think to ask about aircraft noise.'

Life beneath landing routes is worst in those areas situated beneath aerial crossroads. The north London borough of Waltham Forest, for instance, is well away from Heathrow by car or bus, but is the third most overflown London borough, simply because it lies squarely under the point at which the approach routes to Heathrow and City Airport intersect.[80] Airports in such close proximity do not only cause problems down on the ground. Up in the air, their controlled airspace merges into vast, restricted swathes of sky like the huge British estates that in the late eighteenth century enclosed moorland and pasture to which there had been public access for centuries.

The commercial airliners for whose use Britain's airways and other controlled airspace exists doubtless seem like an innumerable legion to those living beneath their flight paths. In fact, though, they make up less than 10 per cent of the traffic using Britain's skies. 'General aviation' is an umbrella term that covers everything else (apart from military aircraft): from hang-gliders to air taxis, from hot-air balloons to helicopters. It includes approximately 14,000 powered aircraft, 1,600 balloons, more than 2,000 gliders and around 4,500 hang-gliders. In addition to these, roughly 4,500 parachutists regularly drop through the country's ether.[81] These communities of air users are in many ways the pedestrians, the cyclists, the quad bike riders of Britain's skies, flying mostly in the margins of the country's controlled airspace, under, around and between the great motorway-like flight paths and the busy terminal manoeuvring areas.

Brian Hope of the Light Aircraft Association has been flying recreationally since the 1970s and has owned his own small plane for 25 years. 'Flying is not just something that rich people do,' he insists. 'For most of my life I was an ordinary Joe on a building site. Flying covers the whole spectrum of society.'[82] The Light Aircraft Association has more than 8,000 members, many of whom have built or restored their own planes or own a share in a plane syndicate. The association was set up in the wake of the Second World War, with the aim of making flying affordable to the man on the street – many of whom, of course, had learned to fly during the war.[83] Despite the sheer numbers of general air users today, though, the members of the LAA seem to find themselves with a perpetually shrinking share of Britain's skies.

'Every year,' Brian Hope explains, 'Britain's controlled airspace grows. General aviation is the poor relation. When commercial air traffic wants to get more controlled airspace, it tends to get it. In the last twenty years, it has gone completely mad. And the controlled airspace has grown like a jigsaw puzzle, with bits added here and there. It's not the most efficient use of the space.' This is a concern shared by other general aviation pilots. Most blame the fact that in recent years more and more provincial airports have asked for controlled airspace above them. 'There are more flights per day taking off from Breighton airfield than from Doncaster airport,' Mickey Kaye sighs, 'yet Doncaster has got a huge chunk of controlled airspace above it now.'[84] The watchdog surveying Britain's skies, the Civil Aviation Authority, is well aware of these concerns and is currently reviewing the map of Britain's airspace, so radical changes to the map of our country's skies could be made in the next decades. 'Hopefully,' Brian Hope says, 'they will release some of the airspace back to general aviation.'[85]

The practical problem with so much free airspace being gobbled up is that it makes routes across the country more and more difficult for general aviation. 'Where I live in the south-east,' Brian Hope says, 'you can fly between airports at the moment to get north or west. But if Farnborough and Southend airports both get controlled airspace, that would block those routes.'[86] It's a little like a gated community suddenly being built in the middle of the Pennine Way or halfway round the South West Coast Path. And it's not just close to London that these problems exist. The controlled airspace around Birmingham and Manchester is also notoriously difficult to avoid, and Bristol's controlled airspace has recently been joined up with Cardiff's to create a vast impasse in the west.

In theory, general air traffic can enter some of Britain's controlled airspace. However, the pilot must request clearance just ten minutes before reaching it; if this is granted, they can enter, provided they do so at precisely the right height, time and bearing, and as long as they are carrying a working radio and transponder (to identify the plane on radar). The problem arises when clearance is refused, or air traffic controllers simply don't respond to the pilot in time. Then, with the boundary of the controlled airspace hard upon them, the only options are to turn back or else try to edge around it like a minefield. For general aviation pilots, the map of Britain's skies has decided 'black spots' in it – airports notorious for refusing clearance, air control towers that never respond. In recent years, though, the aerial equivalents of motorway underpasses have been created at some sites. Manchester Airport now has a 'low level route' passing through its controlled airspace, which can be traversed by private pilots without the need for clearance.[87]

If pilots enter controlled airspace without clearance, they could face a large fine or even the suspension of their licence. Every year, the Civil Aviation Authority publishes a long list of air infringements, and how they were dealt with, which makes sobering reading. The cases that reach the desks of the CAA, though, are only those that were reported. It is estimated that an airspace infringement actually takes places every 11 hours above the UK.[88] Most of them seem genuinely to happen by mistake – in the air, there are no 'Private Property' signs, no barricades, just painstaking map-reading. In recent years, however, the situation has been helped enormously by the widespread use of GPS. 'GPS has changed the face of aerial navigation,' Brian Hope says. 'It will give you a warning as you're approaching controlled airspace and will literally guide you around the edge if necessary.'[89]

GPS technology is also invaluable to those pilots who keep well away from airways and airport control zones – to those who fly exclusively in Britain's 'uncontrolled airspace', where they are responsible for finding their own way, and for keeping themselves safely separated from any other aircraft. The vast majority of sport and recreational pilots tend to stick within these aerial common lands, despite the alarming rate at which they are shrinking. Indeed, many pride themselves on having nothing to do with air traffic controllers.

There are still regions of Britain that have few airways above them, where it is easy to be a free-ranging aeronautical rambler. Cornwall has just two airways crossing its upper airspace and none in its lower airspace. Both West Wales and North Yorkshire, similarly, are open aerial territory up to 24,500 feet. And although the Western Highlands and the far north of Scotland are criss-crossed by flight paths above 24,500 feet, below that level they have wide empty skies. The downside of flying in such areas, however, is that routes have to be more carefully planned as fewer airways also often means fewer places to refuel, or to land in an emergency.

The other – and more common – way of avoiding controlled airspace is simply to fly beneath it. This is obviously easier in some areas than in others – most of greater London has controlled airspace above it from 2,500 feet upwards. But flying relatively low in Britain's skies involves its own hazards and obstacles. Pilots must beware of sudden high ground, radio masts, wind turbines, and even model aircraft. They need to avoid gliding sites, military training areas, small airfields, and – at certain times of the year – bird reserves. General aviation pilots are also warned never to fly at an altitude of between 250 and 500 feet because it is at that height band that most military low flying takes place.[90]

I ask Brian Hope whether, with all of these restrictions, Britain's skies still offer anything of the freedom they must have held for Vincenzo Lunardi on that day in 1784 when the whole of the British heavens were spread out before him like a glorious untrodden field of snow. 'You certainly still get a sense of space and freedom,' he says. 'As soon as you leave the ground, the world opens up. It's funny,' he muses, 'but it always amazes me how quickly you're alone. You might get 1,000 aircraft at a weekend event, and at the end of the Sunday they all take off one after the other into the air. But within five to ten miles, all of those people have disappeared off in different directions. The sky's a very big place.'[91]

General aviation pilots fly above Britain for all kinds of reasons, but it hardly ever seems to be purely a way of getting from A to B. 'There are usually philosophical and personal reasons,' Brian Hope says. 'It's the ultimate way of getting away from your troubles – perfect escapism.'[92] Flying, it seems, shrinks Britain – making the Isle of Wight just a short day trip from London – but also unfolds unsuspected space, both literal and metaphysical.

On the one hand, the pilot's map of Britain reveals a region that can seem depressingly developed, legislated and teeming, with its contested borders, its increasing reliance on technology, and its clustering airways mirroring our busiest motorways. On the other hand, it seems that there will always be room within that map for the old dream of the sky as a glorious void. In a country that often feels crowded, Britain's skies will probably forever remain a symbol of our desire for escape. But what we might learn from the enterprising general aviation pilots who edge around our heavens is that no matter how congested the place you inhabit, it only takes perseverance and imagination for there to be space for everyone.

Afterword

In a sense, this is a book with no ending. For every chapter here, countless others could have been written. Chapter One explored the cavers' map of Britain. But what does the map of the country's Cold War nuclear shelters look like? Its carefully protected heart lies on the edge of the Cotswolds, close to the market town of Corsham (where a 35-acre underground facility was once kept at the ready to house 4,000 government personnel if necessary). But for the 1,000 plus members of Subterranea Britannica, a society dedicated to rediscovering such sites, Burlington Bunker is just one buried treasure on a pirates' map that stretches from Scotland to Cornwall.

Chapter Two traced the distribution of megaliths across the country. But what is the shape of Arthurian Britain, and where were (or still are) the country's main monastic centres? And what would Britain look like if, instead of sketching its network of ley lines, we traced its main telecommunications cables, or identified its main radon areas? To borrow a metaphor from the beginning of this book, writing *Britannia Obscura* was a little like caving. There was forever the possibility that just as the uttermost extremities of one system were reached, a whole new set of beginnings would surprisingly open up, waiting to be explored. So before I accidentally stumble upon a Titan, it is time to put down the shovel and briefly reflect.

Had the telecommunications chart, the Arthurian map of Britain, or the distribution of radon-affected areas been traced in this book, then yet more new shapes would have materialised within the borders of our country, like old paintings hidden beneath the oils of a familiar landscape. But surprising coincidences might also have emerged. Cornwall, for instance, would have featured not just as a key site for megalith hunters, on account of its multiple stone circles, but also as a radon hotspot. And it would have assumed importance not only as the crossing point of the long-distance Michael ley line with the international Apollo and Athena line, but also as the place at which Britain's internet connection feeds into the country from New York – via a vast submarine cable coincidentally known as Apollo North.[1] This would have happily reinforced one of the book's main messages – that our categories of rural and urban are artificial constructs, and one person's sleepy, remote and unexceptional province is the busy centre of another's map. However, it might also have been in danger of appearing to simply replace one centre with another – London with Cornwall – and that is not at all the point of this book, which aims rather to argue that there is no one centre, no absolute peripheries, and no objective borders.

The map-maker and author Tim Robinson has said that he always felt, growing up in Yorkshire and then living on the west coast of Ireland, that he lived 'on the fold of the map'.[2] The aim of this book is to argue that, whether you live in Conway or in Coventry, you will always be at the centre of somebody's idea of the shape of Britain. For this reason, I have tried to spread the focus of the book geographically across the country, as far as possible. However, some bias will inevitably remain, simply because I live and work in the south-west, because I grew up in Yorkshire, and because I once lived in Cumbria, and so will always unavoidably be drawn to sites in those areas, like a hedgehog following its nightly peregrinations.

The problem of subjectivity is one reason why this book, although ostensibly written by one person, has included maps and stories and routes around the country that have been generously shared by numerous individuals, making it in some sense a joint work, created by us all. I have also tried, in selecting material, to present Britain through a variety of lenses – some focused very locally, others viewing the country's place within a broader, world-wide context. So attention has deliberately moved between the story of one man discovering ancient stones in his own parish, the very national narrative of Britain's canal-building, and the international history of man's attempts to fly, as a reminder that any map we might make of Britain will always be part of a larger map – and also a composite and simplification of smaller, more detailed local maps.

The inevitable simplification of maps, their unavoidable bias and politics, and their aesthetics and conventions are all subjects that have been theorised over the years by geographers, historians, philosophers and political theorists. They have analysed the relationship of maps to the workings of power, the relationship between spatial communities and communities of interest, and the role of imagined geographies in the formation of identity.[3] This book has touched lightly on some of those issues. But it is not a book that is interested in the abstract. It is a book that hopes to inspire exploration – not just in the mind, but on the ground, under the ground, on the water and in the air. A book that will be happiest if it is crumpled in a rucksack, muddied in a footwell, or dropped accidentally over the side of a canal boat. Ultimately, it is a book that aims to make its readers more familiar with the shape of Britain, but also perpetually and wonderfully surprised by it.

Notes

Introduction: The Shape of Britain

1 In 2007, Newquay was praised as Britain's surf capital by Labour MP Phyllis Starkey and has since marketed itself using that title. See Sam Jefferson, 'Newquay Praised as Beacon Seaside Town', *Newquay Voice*, 14 March, 2007, www.newquayvoice.co.uk. The Cornish village of Braunton with its surf museum also claims that it is 'one of Britain's surf capitals', www.barnstablechamber.co.uk.

2 Information taken from the species richness maps produced by Butterfly Conservation, www.butterfly-conservation.org.

3 The first attempt to map Britain's birds was made in 1950 by Tony Norris but examined only the West Midlands. See Tony Norris, *West Midland Bird Distribution Survey* (published for private circulation, 1960).

4 The project was organised by the British Trust for Ornithology, www.bto.org.

5 Henry Mayhew, *London Labour and the London Poor: A Cyclopaedia of the Condition and Earnings of Those That Will Work, Those That Cannot Work, and Those That Will Not Work* (London: Griffin, Bohn and co., 1861), p.454.

6 See www.police.uk.

7 See R.C. Richardson, 'William Camden and the Re-Discovery of England', *Transactions of the Leicestershire Archaeological and Historical Society*, 78 (2004), pp.108-123.

8 This case was argued in an edition of the Scottish hillwalking

fanzine, *The Angry Corrie*. See *The Angry Corrie*, 25 (November 1995 – January 1996), www.keswick.u-net.com/hillinfo.

9 Timothy Darvill, *Prehistoric Britain* (Abingdon: Routledge, 1987), p.245.

10 This is the view of author and enthusiast of Hadrian's Wall, Mark Richards, who runs the 'Hadrian's Triumph' charity enterprise and has written the definitive walkers' guide to the wall, (interview with Mark Richards, 20/01/12).

11 See Stuart McHardy, 'A New History of Scotland, Part 2: They Came, They Saw, They Left', www.newsnetscotland.co.uk.

12 See John Carvel, 'North-south, east-west wealth divides in survey', *Guardian*, 10 November 2005, www.theguardian.com; Phil Thornton, 'House Prices: The East-West Divide', *Independent*, 16 April, 2008, www.independent.co.uk.

13 See Francis Pryor, *Britain AD: A Quest for Arthur, England and the Anglo-Saxons* (London: Harper Collins, 2004), p.129.

Chapter One: Underground, Overground: The Caver's Map of Britain

1. See John Hutton, p.259, on 18th-century claims.
2. See Hewitt, pp.137–48.
3. See Beck, pp.25–8.
4. Quoted in ibid., p.32.
5. Quoted in ibid.
6. Dave Nixon, conversation with the author, 24 January 2011.
7. See www.ukcaves.co.uk for fuller description of the system.
8. Andy Walsh, conversation with the author, 24 April 2014.
9. See Balderston, pp.69–70.
10. Cornes, p.18.
11. See ibid., p.19.
12. Corrected length published in *Descent* 215 (August 2010).
13. Tarquin Wilton-Jones, conversation with the author, 11 February 2011.
14. Tarquin Wilton-Jones, conversation with the author, 11 February 2011.
15. Tarquin Wilton-Jones, conversation with the author, 11 February 2011.

16. Dave Brook predicted this in the 1968 University of Leeds Speleological Club journal, quoted in 'Breakthrough Connection Unites Counties in UK's Longest Cave System', Red Rose and Pothole Club Press Release, 8 November 2011.

17. Andy Walsh, 'The Earby Pump', *Descent* 224 (2012), p.20. See also Tim Allen, 'The Final Piece of the Jigsaw', *Descent* 224 (2012), pp.18–23.

18. Tim Allen, 'The Final Piece of the Jigsaw', *Descent* 224 (2012), p.23.

19. Hugh St Lawrence, quoted in 'Breakthrough Connection Unites Counties in UK's Longest Cave System', Red Rose and Pothole Club Press Release, 8 November 2011.

20. Wilton-Jones.

21. Dave Nixon, conversation with the author, 24 January 2011.

22. Chris Jewell, conversation with the author, 25 January 2011.

23. Chris Jewell, conversation with the author, 25 January 2011.

24. See, for instance, posts by the University of Leeds Speleological Association, http://www.ulsa.org.uk/rants/index.php.

25. Andy Hall, 'Notes on the Early Investigations on Casterton and Leck Fell', website of the Red Rose Cave and Pothole Club, http://www.rrcpc.org.uk/easegill/text/Early–History.htm.

26. The Council of Northern Caving Clubs controls access to Leck Fell and issues permits a minimum of three months before trips underground. See http://cncc.org.uk/about/leck-fell-faqs.php.

27. Dave Nixon, conversation with the author, 24 January 2011.

28. Tarquin Wilton-Jones, conversation with the author, 11 February 2011.

29. Description of the Mendips underground region from University of Leeds Speleological Society, http://www.ubss.org.uk/UK–caving–areas.php.

30. 'Fact Sheet 8: Rivers', *Cheddar Caves and Gorge Discovery Pack* (2001).

31. Gavin Newman, 'Time Tunnel: The Exploration of Wookey Hole Cave', *Dive Magazine* www.divemagazine.co.uk.

32. Ibid.

33. Ibid.

34. www.ubss.ac.uk.

35. James Plumptre, excerpted in Ousby p.65.

36. See Oldham.

37. Ibid., p.26.
38. See Smith, pp.32–3.
39. It was published in Catcott, p.38. On this subject see also Mullan.
40. Quoted in Catcott, p.40.
41. Quoted in ibid., p.292.
42. Mullan, p.294; Catcott, p.41.
43. Catcott, p.33.
44. Ibid., p.11.
45. J. S. Chamberlain, 'Alexander Catcott', *ODNB*.
46. Catcott, p.29.
47. Ibid., p.47.
48. John Hutton, pp.250, 244, 246.
49. Ibid., p.246.
50. Anon., p.471.
51. John Hutton, p.247.
52. Ibid., p.255.
53. Ibid., p.263.
54. Burke outlined his aesthetic theories in his 1757 work *A Philosophical Enquiry into the Origin of our Ideas of the Sublime and Beautiful.*
55. John Hutton, p.253.
56. Exton, pp.3–8.
57. See Plumptre, in Ousby, pp.67–8.
58. Ibid., p.69.
59. Ibid., p.71.
60. Ibid.
61. Ousby.
62. Ford, p.62.
63. Wilton-Jones.
64. Ibid.
65. Dave Nixon, conversation with the author, 24 January 2011.
66. Wilton-Jones.
67. Andy Walsh, conversation with the author, 24 April 2014.
68. Tarquin Wilton-Jones, conversation with the author, 11 February 2011.
69. BBC interview, 8 November 2006, www.bbc.co.uk.
70. Dave Nixon, conversation with the author, 24 January 2011.
71. Emma Lidiard, 'Caves to Link Cumbria, Lancashire and Yorkshire',

Westmorland Gazette, 12 August 2010, www.thewestmorlandgazette. co.uk.

72. Andy Hall, 'Notes on the Early Investigations on Casterton and Leck Fell', website of the Red Rose Cave and Pothole Club, http://www.rrcpc.org.uk/easegill/text/Early–History.htm.

73. www.ukcaves.co.uk.

74. Cornes, p.20.

75. See ibid.

76. Wilton-Jones.

77. Ibid.

Chapter Two: Prehistoric Patterns: The Megalithic Shape of Britain

1. Timothy Darvill, conversation with the author, 1 March 2011.

2. For instance, Taylor. See Burl, *Stone Circles of Britain*, p.72, on this.

3. Burl, *Great Stone Circles*, pp.88, 81.

4. Darvill, *Prehistoric Britain*, p.67.

5. Ibid., p.68.

6. Ibid.

7. This is a widely disseminated story. See, for instance, www.ikbrunel. org.uk/boxtunnel. It is, however, discounted in C.P. Atkins, 'Box Railway Tunnel and I. K. Brunel's Birthday – a Theoretical Investigation', *Journal of the British Astronomical Association*, 95:6 (October 1985), 260.

8. Darvill, *Prehistoric Britain*, p.53.

9. Ibid., p.67.

10. Timothy Darvill, conversation with the author, 1 March 2011.

11. Hayman, pp.8, 13.

12. Ibid., p.12.

13. See the Atmospheric Haunted Places blogspot, 14 February 2009, http://atmospherichauntedplaces.blogspot.co.uk.

14. Comment at https://heritageaction.wordpress.com.

15. 'Keith', 'Pagan Encroachment on Wiltshire's Ancient Sites', the Anti Pagan Coalition on www.facebook.com.

16. See Cope, p.223.

17. www.warband.org.uk.

18. Darvill, *Prehistoric Britain*, p.94.

19. Burl, *From Carnac to Callanish*, p.14.

20. See Chippendale, pp.196, 232.

21. See Darvill, *Prehistoric Britain*, p.94.

22. See www.ivanmcbeth.com.

23. The Megalithic Portal, forum, 1 March 2011, www.megalithic.co.uk.

24. See www.ivanmcbeth.com.

25. Philip Carr-Gomm, conversation with the author, 3 March 2011.

26. See, for instance, www.hedgeDruid.com.

27. See Chippendale, pp.264–71.

28. Burl, *Stone Circles of Britain*, p.36.

29. Burl, *Great Stone Circles*, p.167; Burl, *Stone Circles of Britain*, p.36.

30. See Burl, *Great Stone Circles*, p.101.

31. See Chippendale, p.20; Burl, *Great Stone Circles*, p.102.

32. See Chippendale, p.2.

33. See Ronald Hutton, 'Megaliths and Memory', p.12; Cadbury, pp.1–9.

34. See Ronald Hutton, 'Megaliths and Memory', p.14.

35. See Hayman, pp.41–2. For accounts of stones from this period see, for instance, Gibson, pp.6, 10.

36. See Hayman, p.5.

37. Chippendale, p.48.

38. Hayman, p.42.

39. Chippendale, p.60.

40. Ibid., pp.61, 64. See also Hill for more on this subject.

41. See Hayman, pp.47–50.

42. Ibid., p.52.

43. Chippendale, p.70.

44. Ronald Hutton, 'Megaliths and Memory', p.13.

45. Hayman, p.47.

46. Ibid., p.60.

47. Ronald Hutton, *Druids*, p.54.

48. Stukeley, *Abury*, p.51.

49. Ibid., p.63.

50. Hayman, p.68.

51. Ronald Hutton, 'Megaliths and Memory', p.15.

52. See Smiles, p.82; Ronald Hutton, *Blood and Mistletoe*, pp.105, 163–8.

53. Stukeley, *Stonehenge*, pp.2, 40, 56.

54. Borlase, p.127.
55. Ibid., p.199.
56. 'Jerusalem', in Blake, p.39; Wordsworth, p.123; Paas, p.4.
57. See Ronald Hutton, 'Megaliths and Memory', p.18; Hayman, p.116.
58. Ronald Hutton, *Blood and Mistletoe*, p.333.
59. Ronald Hutton, *Druids*, pp.140–41.
60. Ibid., pp.150–51.
61. Ibid., p.174.
62. Ibid., p.189. For a full account of Stonehenge's twentieth-century relationship with neo-Druids, see Worthington.
63. Burl, *Great Stone Circles*, p.146.
64. Ibid.
65. See ibid., p.149; Darvill, *Prehistoric Britain*, p.97.
66. See Orme, p.218.
67. Burl, *Stone Circles of Britain*, p.173.
68. Ibid., p.65.
69. See ibid., p.31; www.heritageaction.wordpress.com.
70. Burl, *Stone Circles of Britain*, pp.33–42, 78.
71. See Darvill, *Prehistoric Britain*, p.86; Philip Carr Gomm, quoted on OBOD website, www.druidry.org.
72. Andy Burnham, owner of the Megalithic Portal, with input from his team of volunteers, conversation with the author, 9 March 2011.
73. Ronald Hutton, quoted on OBOD website, www.druidry.org.
74. Joanne Parker, interview with Andy Burnham, 9 March 2011.
75. Cope, p.ix.
76. Ibid., pp.47–55; 135–9.
77. See ibid., pp.73–87.
78. Burl, *Stone Circles of Britain*, p.68.
79. See Cope, especially p.70.
80. Burl, *Stone Circles of Britain*, p.68.
81. Timothy Darvill, conversation with author, 1 March 2011.
82. David Keys, 'Found after 4,000 Years: The Lost Wooden Sister of Stonehenge', *Independent*, 22 June 2010, www.independent.co.uk.
83. Timothy Darvill, conversation with the author, 1 March 2011.
84. Burl, *Stone Circles of Britain*, p.164.
85. See Chippendale, pp.192–3.
86. Burl, *Stone Circles of Britain*, p.77.

87.   Ibid., p.37.

88.   Ibid., p.226.

89.   Ibid., p.175.

90.   Timothy Darvill, conversation with the author, 1 March 2011.

91.   Timothy Darvill, conversation with the author, 1 March 2011.

92.   James Sturcke and Maeve Kennedy, '"Second Stonehenge" Discovered Near Original', *Guardian*, 6 October 2009, www.theguardian.com.

93.   Burl, *Great Stone Circles*, p.76.

94.   Cope, p.70.

95.   Ibid., p.71.

96.   www.themodernantiquarian.com, blogsite.

97.   Hayman, pp.22–3.

98.   Polwhele, p.146.

99.   Ibid., p.147.

100.   Ibid., pp.140, 147, 154.

101.   Bray, pp.60–61.

102.   Ibid., pp.6, 52.

103.   Stukeley, *Abury*, p.16.

104.   interview with Andy Burnham, conversation with the author, 9 March 2011.

105.   Darvill, *Prehistoric Britain*, p.14.

106.   Burke, p.77.

107.   Doolittle, p.491.

Chapter Three: Hidden Highways:
The Lost Map of Britain's Inland Navigators

1.   Iolo Morganwg, quoted in 'Cardiff City and County (Caerdydd)', Davies et al., in/web. 14 April 2011.

2.   See Russell, pp.108–11.

3.   See Dan O'Neil, 'Lost Canal That's Only Now Missed', *South Wales Echo*, 8 February 2011, www.walesonline.co.uk.

4.   www.flickr.com/photos/stuartherbert.

5.   In 1947, the British Transport Commission took over 2,064 miles of canal – the majority of Britain's inland waterways, with just a few exceptions such as the Manchester Ship Canal. See Squires, p.21.

6. Fisher, p.5.
7. Ibid., p.140.
8. Joanne Parker, interview with Sue Day, 11 October 2011.
9. Boughey and Hadfield, p.52.
10. Sue Day, conversation with the author, 11 October 2011.
11. Sue Day, conversation with the author, 11 October 2011.
12. Sue Day, conversation with the author, 11 October 2011.
13. Fisher, p.163.
14. Ibid., p.164.
15. Ibid., p.165. See also www.canaljunction.com.
16. Fisher, p.165.
17. Squires, p.6.
18. Hopkins, p.26.
19. These were erected by Birmingham Canal Navigations, a registered charity, in 1983. See www.bcnsociety.co.uk.
20. Freeman, p.3.
21. See Fisher, p.40.
22. Ibid.
23. Boughey and Hadfield, pp.230–31; Fisher, p.41.
24. www.canalmuseum.org.uk/history/ukcanals.htm.
25. Fisher, p.296.
26. Ibid., p.282.
27. Russell, p.17.
28. www.shirecruisers.co.uk/routes/one-way-routes.htm.
29. Fisher, p.209.
30. Crowden, p.135; Fisher, p.223.
31. Fisher, p.223.
32. Ibid., p.46.
33. Boughey and Hadfield, p.47.
34. Ibid., pp.47-8.
35. Fisher, p.177.
36. Ibid., p.296.
37. Ibid., p.196; Crowden, p.85.
38. Boughey and Hadfield, p.25; Fisher, p.280.
39. Boughey and Hadfield, p.25.
40. Crowden, p.81; Boughey and Hadfield, p.26.
41. Boughey and Hadfield, p.27; Fisher, p.196; Crowden, p.82.

42. Boughey and Hadfield, p.30.

43. www.icons.org.uk.

44. Crowden, p.82.

45. Boughey and Hadfield, p.30; Fisher, p.207.

46. Fisher, p.199.

47. Ibid.; Crowden, p.82.

48. Boughey and Hadfield, p.93.

49. Squires, p.7.

50. Crowden, p.81.

51. Squires, p.6.

52. Fisher, p. 114; Boughey and Hadfield, p.116.

53. Boughey and Hadfield, p.117.

54. See, for instance, ibid., on the Grand Western Canal.

55. Fisher, p.50.

56. Boughey and Hadfield, p.82.

57. Crowden, p.76; www.icons.org.uk.

58. Crowden, p.88.

59. Boughey and Hadfield, p.34.

60. Russell, p.26.

61. Body and Gallop, p.32.

62. See www.iwa.com; Fisher, pp.170, 274.

63. Squires, p.6.

64. Ibid., p.7.

65. Ibid.

66. Boughey and Hadfield, p.174.

67. Squires, p.7.

68. Boughey and Hadfield, p.175.

69. Ibid., p.181.

70. Squires, p.8.

71. Boughey and Hadfield, p.180.

72. Squires, p.9.

73. Ibid.

74. Ibid., p.12.

75. Crowden, p.89.

76. Roger Squires, conversation with the author, 29 September 2011.

77. Fisher, p.240.

78. www.theaa.com.

79. Squires, pp.13, 172.

80. Ibid., p.18.

81. Ibid.

82. Ibid., p.128.

83. Roger Squires, conversation with the author, 29 September 2011.

84. Squires, pp.71, 77.

85. Ibid., p.89.

86. Ibid., pp.102, 111, 115.

87. Ibid., pp.139, 179.

88. See www.canaljunction.com; Squires, p.152.

89. Fisher, p.287.

90. Ian Herbert, 'Longest Canal Tunnel to Reopen Route Through Pennines after 50 Years', *Independent*, 28 October 1999, www.independent.co.uk.

91. See www.cotswoldcanals.com.

92. See www.iwa.com; Russell, p.23.

93. Squires, p.175.

94. See, for instance, letter from B. James, *South Wales Echo*, 10 January 2011, www.walesonline.co.uk.

95. Squires, p.177.

96. Tony Lewery, 'Upsetting Applecarts', www.canaljunction.com, October 2004; Tony Lewery, 'Concerning Conservation', www.canaljunction.com, May 2005.

97. Tony Lewery, 'With Retrospect', www.canaljunction.com, October 2010; Tony Lewery, 'Concerning Conservation', www.canaljunction.com, May 2005.

98. Tony Lewery, 'Upsetting Applecarts', www.canaljunction.com, October 2004.

99. Squires, p.180.

100. See, for instance, Fisher, p.207, for an account of the Bridgewater Canal's progress.

101. Ibid., p.41.

Chapter Four: Lines Across the landscape:
The Ley Hunter's Map of Britain

1. Television viewing figures from www.therugbyplayer.com.
2. The national grid is made up of 4,500 miles of overhead cable and 450 miles of underground cable (www.nationalgrid.com).
3. Devereux and Thomson, pp.160, 190; Poulton-Smith, p.84; Street, p.90.
4. Michell, *New View Over Atlantis*, p.73.
5. Street, p.8; Neal, p.11.
6. Street, p.7.
7. Stout, p.173.
8. Watkins, *Early British Trackways*, p.viii.
9. Ibid., p.5.
10. Ibid.
11. Ibid., pp.40, 33.
12. Ibid., p.16.
13. Ibid., pp.59, 2.
14. Ibid., p.11.
15. Watkins, quoted in Devereux, *New Ley Hunter's Guide*, p.31. See also Watkins, *Ley Hunter's Manual*, p.69.
16. Watkins, *Early British Trackways*, p.11.
17. Williamson and Bellamy, p.81.
18. Ibid., p.63.
19. Watkins, *Old Straight Track*, p.211; Watkins, quoted in Stout, p.202.
20. Quoted in Stout, p.183.
21. Ibid., p.188.
22. See ibid., pp.189, 181. Only four out of 37 reviewers of *The Old Straight Track* were unimpressed or sarcastic.
23. Watkins, *Old Straight Track*, p.149.
24. Stout, p.178.
25. Belloc, quoted in Stout, p.178.
26. Quoted in Williamson and Bellamy, p.14.
27. See Stout, p.186.
28. Ibid., pp.214, 186.
29. Ibid., pp.192–5.

30. Ibid., pp.200–2.

31. Ibid., p.200.

32. Michell, *New View Over Atlantis*, pp.29, 32.

33. Quoted by John Michell, 'Introduction', in Watkins, *Ley Hunter's Manual*, 1983, p.6.

34. Poulton-Smith, pp.9, 7.

35. Allen Watkins, quoted in Michell, *New View Over Atlantis*, p.23.

36. Ibid.

37. Stout, p.213; Williamson and Bellamy, p.14.

38. Williamson and Bellamy, p.15.

39. Ibid.

40. Michell, *New View Over Atlantis*, p.84.

41. Ibid., p.93.

42. Ibid., pp.88–90.

43. Ibid., pp.44–6.

44. See Williamson and Bellamy, p.18.

45. Ibid., p.85.

46. Ibid., p.128.

47. Ibid., p.15.

48. Ibid., p.25.

49. Most notably in Steve Hillage's single 'Ley-lines to Glassdom' (Virgin, 1977).

50. See Butler, p.132.

51. Michell, *New View Over Atlantis*, p.97.

52. Ibid., p.50.

53. Devereux and Thomson, p.9.

54. Ibid.

55. Michell, *New View Over Atlantis*, p.97.

56. Devereux and Thomson, pp.42–3.

57. Quoted in ibid., p.42.

58. Ibid., pp.43, 38.

59. Williamson and Bellamy, p.211.

60. Michell, *New View Over Atlantis*, p.31.

61. Street, p.1.

62. See Williamson and Bellamy, p.151.

63. See www.leyhunter.org.

64. Ibid.

65. Eric Sargeant, conversation with the author, 12 April 2013.

66. Watkins, *Early British Trackways*, p.5.

67. See, for instance, Devereux, *New Ley Hunter's Guide*, p.139.

68. See ibid., pp.87, 90; Street, pp.21–72.

69. Michell, *New View Over Atlantis*, p.76.

70. Broadhurst and Miller, pp.39, 125, 139, 47.

71. Ibid., p.25.

72. Ibid., pp.39, 188.

73. See www.belinusline.com.

74. See, for instance, www.dowsingaustralia.com, for details of François Capmeil's series of pilgrimages from Australia in the 1990s.

75. Richard Dealler, *Mary Michael Pilgrims Way: Brentor to Glastonbury* (Exeter: privately printed, 2011). See www.marymichaelpilgrimsway.org.

76. Williamson and Bellamy, pp.150, 151.

77. Ibid., p.150.

78. Devereux and Thomson, p.37.

79. See, for instance, Devereux, *New Ley Hunter's Guide*, p.117. On the Land's End ley lines and statistics, see ibid., p.43, and Bellamy and Williamson, p.105.

80. See Watkins, *Old Straight Track*, p.195.

81. Timpson, p.156.

82. Ibid., p.190.

83. Street, p.92.

84. Ibid., pp.98, 96.

85. Poulton-Smith, pp.20, 21, 78, 84.

86. Ibid., pp.46, 72, 73.

87. Watkins, *Ley Hunter's Manual*, p.94.

88. Street, p.194.

89. Neal, p.27.

90. Ibid., p.29.

91. Ibid., pp.30–32.

92. Ibid., pp.14, 21.

93. Broadhurst and Miller, pp.63, 129, 78.

94. www.dowsingaustralia.com.

95. See, for instance, Broadhurst and Miller, pp.39, 41.

96. *Telegraph*, 8 November 2007, www.thetelegraph.co.uk.

97. Timpson, p.150.

98. Christopher Street, conversation with the author, 12 April 2013.

99. Grahame Gardner, conversation with the author, 6 April 2013.

100. John Christian, conversation with the author, 2 April 2013.

101. Broadhurst and Miller, p.122.

102. Ibid., p.104.

103. Poulton-Smith, p.112.

104. Devereux and Thomson, p.201.

105. Williamson and Bellamy, p.146.

106. Timpson, p.9.

107. Watkins, *Old Straight Track*, p.222; Devereux and Thomson, p.44.

108. John Christian, conversation with the author, 2 April 2013.

109. Street, p.200.

Chapter Five: Highways in the Air: The Map of Britain's Skies

1.   Of the three accounts of this incident, only one names Athelstan as the enemy. The date of the battle varies. For a very full account of the different versions of the story, see Hall, and Ash. On the flag of St Andrew, see also Groom, pp.84–8.

2.   www.nats.co.uk.

3.   Michael Lyddon, conversation with the author, 5 August 2013.

4.   Peter Gill, conversation with the author, 3 August 2013.

5.   See ENR 6-3-1-1, published by the CAA, 7 March 2013; and ENR 6-3-1-2, published by the CAA, 10 January 2013.

6.   Ibid.

7.   www.nats.co.uk.

8.   See ENR 6-1-7-1, published by the CAA, 13 December 2012.

9.   www.nats.co.uk.

10. See Holmes, pp.16–20.

11. According to an unnamed correspondent in the *Morning Post and Advertiser*, 12 August 1784.

12. See the *Morning Herald and Daily Advertiser*, 16 September 1784; the *General Evening Post*, 16 September 1784. See Holmes, p.24, on Horace Walpole's outrage regarding the cat.

13. The *Morning Herald* had described the balloon in this way on 2 August 1784, when plans for the flight were first announced. On the crowds watching the balloon, see the *Morning Herald and Daily Advertiser*, 16 September 1784.

14. See the *London Chronicle*, 17 September 1784; the *General Evening Post*, 16 September 1784; the *Morning Herald and Daily Advertiser*, 16 September 1784.

15. Jean-Pierre Blanchard.

16. See Holmes, pp.53–8.

17. *Public Advertiser*, 21 October 1784.

18. See Holmes, pp.6–10, for a full account of this incident.

19. *London Chronicle*, 17 September 1785; *Whitehall Evening Post*, 17 September 1785.

20. The *Public Advertiser*, for instance, asserted after Lunardi's flight: 'they never can be depended on [. . .] they will hardly ever be used, except of a small size for entertainment' (21 October 1784).

21. Holmes, p.22.

22. Ibid., p.76.

23. See ibid., p.52.

24. See the *Birmingham Daily Post*, 26 March 1862, p.4.

25. See Holmes, pp.203–6.

26. *Birmingham Daily Post*, 19 July 1862, p.2.

27. *Birmingham Daily Post*, 1 July 1862, p.4.

28. *Birmingham Daily Post*, 19 July 1862, p.2.

29. Ibid., p.5.

30. *Birmingham Daily Post*, 8 September 1862, p.3; *Birmingham Gazette*, 13 September 1862, p.6.

31. Holmes, p.220.

32. See Brown, p.10; Cooper, p.8.

33. Brown, p.19.

34. Ibid., pp.20–21.

35. Grant, p.14.

36. Ibid., p.57.

37. Brown, p.21; Cooper, p.10.

38. Brown, p.11.

39. Ibid., pp.11, 15.

40. The *Daily Mail* described it in this way. See Brown, p.11.

41.   See Brown, pp.24–6.

42.   See ibid., pp.26, 27; Cooper, p.12.

43.   See Cooper, p.15. In 1996, the tree was removed from its original spot amid protests and was re-sited at the headquarters of the Defence Evaluation Research Agency. Today a concrete embossed image of the tree and a plaque remain on the original site.

44.   See ibid., pp.117, 36.

45.   See ibid., p.18. Among the other memorials on Farnborough Airfield are the Busk Memorial in memory of Edward Busk (see ibid., p.20).

46.   Brown, p.33.

47.   Ibid., pp.36, 72.

48.   Ibid., p.62.

49.   Ibid., pp.86–93.

50.   *Manchester Guardian*, 24 July 1911, p.7.

51.   *Manchester Guardian*, 29 July 1911, p.10.

52.   Brown, p.147.

53.   Grant, pp.68–73.

54.   Ibid., p.74.

55.   Cooper, p.27; Brown, p.147.

56.   Grant, pp.96–100.

57.   Ibid., p.100.

58.   See www.westernfrontassociation.com.

59.   See www.blackpoolinternational.com.

60.   See www.croydononline.org.

61.   Grant, p.206.

62.   www.nats.co.uk; www.croydononline.org.

63.   www.heathrowairport.com.

64.   Figures from www.nats.co.uk.

65.   Ayliffe, pp.79–90.

66.   See 'Introduction', in Walter Blanchard, p.xi.

67.   Kendall, p.241.

68.   See 'Introduction', in Walter Blanchard, p.xi.

69.   Kendall, pp.241–2.

70.   ENR 6-3-1-2, published by the CAA, 10 January 2013; and ENR 6-3-1-1, published by the CAA, 7 March 2013.

71.   www.nats.co.uk.

72.   Ibid.

73. Ibid.

74. www.heathrowairport.com.

75. See ENR 6-3-1-2, published by the CAA, 10 January 2013.

76. See ENR 6-1-4-1, published by the CAA, 28 June 2012.

77. Figures from www.hacan.org.uk.

78. See www.heathrowairport.com.

79. Gwyn Topham, 'Earth Houses give Pupils Refuge from Heathrow Noise', *Guardian*, 22 April 2013, www.guardian.co.uk.

80. www.hacan.org.uk.

81. Figures from General Aviation Awareness Council, www.gaac.org.uk.

82. Brian Hope, conversation with the author, 2 August 2013.

83. www.laa.uk.com.

84. Mickey Kaye, conversation with the author, 3 August 2013.

85. Brian Hope, conversation with the author, 2 August 2013.

86. Brian Hope, conversation with the author, 2 August 2013.

87. www.nats.co.uk.

88. Ibid.

89. Brian Hope, conversation with the author, 2 August 2013.

90. www.nats.co.uk.

91. Brian Hope, conversation with the author, 2 August 2013.

92. Ibid.

Afterword

1. See Warren Pole, 'The Hidden Cables Under a Cornish Beach Feeding the World's Internet', *Daily Mail*, 5 July 2009, www.mailonline.com. See also www.porthcurno.org.uk.

2. Tim Robinson, in interview with Jos Smith. See 'A Step Towards the Earth: Interview with Tim Robinson', in *Politics of Place*, 1 (2013), pp.4–11, 8.

3. See, for instance, Michael Keith and Steve Pile, *Place and the Politics of Identity* (London: Routledge, 1993); Daniel Kemmis, *Community and the Politics of Place* (Norman, OK: University of Oklahoma Press, 1992); John O.E. Clarke, *Remarkable Maps* (London: Conway Maritime Press, 2005); Paul Hindle, *Maps for Historians* (Chichester: Phillimore, 2006).

Selected Bibliography

References to newspaper and online articles, and to government publications, are cited in the notes only.

For consistency, references in the notes to newspaper articles published before 1800 are cited only by publication title and date, as most of these are anonymous and untitled, and most newspapers from that period were short and unpaginated. All can be easily accessed using either *British Newspapers 1600–1900* (Gale) or www.britishnewspaperarchive.co.uk.

Anon., 'Three Sonnets by William Wordsworth', *Blackwood's Edinburgh Magazine* 4 (1819), 471

Ash, Marinell, 'The Adoption of St Andrew as Patron Saint of Scotland', *British Archaeological Association Conference Transactions* 14 (1994), 16–24

Ayliffe, Alec, 'The Development of Airborne Dead-Reckoning', in Walter Blanchard, *Air Navigation: From Balloons to Concorde* (Bognor Regis: Woodfield, 2005)

Balderston, R. and M., *Ingleton, Bygone and Present* (London: Simpkin, Marshall & Co., 1988)

Beck, Howard M., *Gaping Gill: 150 Years of Exploration* (London: Robert Hale, 1984)

Belloc, Hilaire, *The Old Road* (London: Constable, 1921)

Blake, William, *Selections from the Symbolical Poems of William Blake* (New Haven: Yale University Press, 1915)

Blanchard, Jean-Pierre, *Journal and Certificates on the Fourth Voyage of M. Blanchard, who Ascended from the Royal Military Academy, at Chelsea, the 16th of October, 1784, at Nine Minutes Past Twelve O'Clock, and was Accompanied, as far as Sunbury, by John Sheldon . . . and, from Sunbury, Continued his Voyage, Alone, to Rumsey, in Hampshire* (London: privately printed, 1784)

Blanchard, Walter, *Air Navigation: From Balloons to Concorde* (Bognor Regis: Woodfield, 2005)

Body, G., and R. Gallop, *The Glastonbury Canal* (Bristol: Fiducia Press, 2001)

Borlase, William, *Antiquities, Historical and Monumental, of the County of Cornwall,* (London: Baker and Leigh, 1769)

Boughey, Joseph, and Charles Hadfield, *British Canals: The Standard History* (Stroud: Tempus, 2008)

Bray, Anna Eliza, *The Borders of the Tamar and the Tavy*, Vol. I (London: Kent, 1879)

Broadhurst, Paul, and Hamish Miller, *The Sun and the Serpent* (Launceston: Mythos, 1990)

Brown, Timothy C., *Flying with the Larks: The Early Aviation Pioneers of Lark Hill* (Stroud: The History Press, 2013)

Burke, Edmund, *A Philosophical Enquiry into the Origin of our Ideas of the Sublime and Beautiful* (Oxford: Oxford World's Classics, 1998 [1757])

Burl, Aubrey, *Circles of Stone: The Prehistoric Rings of Britain and Ireland* (London: Harvill, 1999)

   From Carnac to Callanish: Prehistoric Stone Rows and Avenues of Britain, Ireland and Brittany (New Haven: Yale University Press, 1993)

   Great Stone Circles (New Haven: Yale University Press, 1999)

   The Stone Circles of Britain, Ireland and Brittany (New Haven: Yale University Press, 2000)

Burton, Anthony, and Derek Pratt, *The Anatomy of Canals: Decline and Renewal* (Stroud: Tempus, 2003)

Butler, Charles, 'Children of the Stones', in Joanne Parker (ed.), *Written on Stone: The Cultural Reception of British Prehistoric Monuments* (Newcastle: Cambridge Scholars, 2009)

Cadbury, Deborah, *The Dinosaur Hunters* (London: Fourth Estate, 2000)

Catcott, George, *A Descriptive Account of a Descent Made into Pen-park Hole, in the Parish of Westbury-upon-Trim, in the County of Gloucester, in the Year 1775* (Bristol: J. Rudhall, 1792)

Chippendale, Christopher, *Stonehenge Complete* (London: Thames and Hudson, 1983)

Clarke, John O. E., *Remarkable Maps* (London: Conway Maritime Press, 2005)

Cooper, Peter J., *Farnborough: 100 Years of British Aviation* (Hinckley: Midland Publishing, 2006),

Cope, Julian, *The Modern Antiquarian: A Pre-Millennial Odyssey through Megalithic Britain* (London: Thorsons, 1998)

Cornes, George, 'The Intrigue Surrounding the Early Exploration of Lancaster Hole and Ease Gill', *Red Rose Cave and Pothole Club Journal*, 5 (n.d.), 18–20

Crouch, Tom D., *Wings: A History of Aviation from Kites to the Space Age* (New York: W. W. Norton, 2004)

Crowden, James, *Waterways* (London: National Trust, 2004)

Darvill, Timothy, *Prehistoric Britain* (Abingdon: Routledge, 1987, 2010)
Stonehenge: The Biography of a Landscape (Stroud: Tempus, 2007)

Davies, John, Nigel Jenkins, Menna Baines, and Peredur I. Lynch, *The Welsh Academy Encyclopedia of Wales* (Cardiff: University of Wales Press, 2008)

Devereux, Paul, *Spirit Roads: An Exploration of Otherworldly Routes* (London: Collins and Brown, 2007)
The New Ley Hunter's Guide (Glastonbury: Gothic Image, 1994)

Devereux, Paul, and Ian Thomson, *The Ley-Hunter's Companion* (London: Thames and Hudson, 1980)

Doolittle, Hilda, 'R.A.F.', in *Collected Poems 1912–1944* (New York: New Directions, 1983)

Evans, Geraint (ed.), *Rattleskull Genius* (Aberystwyth: University of Wales Centre for Advanced Welsh and Celtic Studies, 2005)

Exton, Kay, 'Aestheticism and Athleticism: The Changing Depictions, Pursuits and Visitors in North Craven, 1750–1900', *Journal of the North Craven Heritage Trust* (2007), 3–8

Fells, Richard, *A Visitor's Guide to Underground Britain: Caves, Caverns, Mines, Tunnels, Grottoes* (Exeter: Webb and Bower, 1989)

Fisher, Stuart, *Canals of Britain: A Comprehensive Guide* (London: Aldard Coles Nautical, 2009),

Ford, Trevor D., Untitled, *Cave Science* 19:1 (August 1992), 62

Freeman, Malcolm D., *Smethwick and the BCN* (Sandwell: Smethwick Heritage Centre Trust, 2003)

Gibson, Edmund, *Camden's Britannia* (London: A. Swalle, 1695)

Grant, R. G., *Flight: The Complete History* (London: Dorling Kindersley, 2010)

Groom, Nick, *The Union Jack* (London: Atlantic, 2006)

Hall, Ursula, *St Andrew and Scotland* (St Andrews: University of St Andrews Library, 1994)

Hayman, Richard, *Riddles in Stone: Myths, Archaeology and the Ancient Britons* (London: Hambledon, 1997)

Hewitt, Rachel, *Map of a Nation: A Biography of the Ordnance Survey* (London: Granta, 2010),

Hill, Rosemary, *Stonehenge* (London: Profile, 2008)

Hindle, Paul, *Maps for Historians* (Chichester: Phillimore, 2006)

Holmes, Richard, *Falling Upwards: How We Took to the Air* (London: William Collins, 2013)

Hopkins, Eric, *Birmingham: The First Manufacturing Town in the World, 1760–1840* (London: Weidenfeld & Nicolson, 1989)

Hutton, John, *A Tour to the Caves, in the Environs of Ingleborough and Settle, in the West Riding of Yorkshire* (London: Richardson and Urquhart, 1780)

Hutton, Ronald, *Blood and Mistletoe* (New Haven: Yale University Press, 2009)

The Druids (London: Hambledon Continuum, 2007)

'Megaliths and Memory', in Joanne Parker (ed.), *Written on Stone: The Cultural Reception of Prehistoric Monuments* (Newcastle: Cambridge Scholars, 2009), 10–22

Johnson, Terry, *Hidden Heritage: Discovering Ancient Essex* (Milverton: Capall Bann, 1996)

Keith, Michael, and Steve Pile, *Place and the Politics of Identity* (London: Routledge, 1993)

Kemmis, Daniel, *Community and the Politics of Place* (Norman, OK: University of Oklahoma Press, 1992)

Kendall, Brian, 'The Beginnings of Directional Radio Techniques for Air Navigation, 1910–1940', in Walter Blanchard, *Air Navigation: From Balloons to Concorde* (Bognor Regis: Woodfield, 2005)

Lesser, Wendy, *The Life Below the Ground: A Study of the Subterranean in Literature and History* (London: Faber and Faber, 1987)

Macfarlane, Rob, *Mountains of the Mind: A History of a Fascination* (London: Granta, 2003)

Mayhew, Henry, *London Labour and the London Poor: A Cyclopaedia of the Condition and Earnings of Those That Will Work, Those That Cannot Work, and Those That Will Not Work* (London: Griffin, Bohn and Co., 1861)

Michell, John, *Megalithomania: Artists, Antiquarians and Archaeologists at the Old Stone Monuments* (London: Thames and Hudson, 1982)
The New View over Atlantis (London: Thames and Hudson, 1986)

Mullan, G. J., 'Pen Park Hole, Bristol: A Reassessment', *The Proceedings of the University of Bristol Speleological Society* 19:3 (1993), 291–311

Neal, Alan, *Ley Lines of the South West* (Ilkley: Bossiney Books, 2004)

Oldham, Tony and Anne, *Discovering Caves: A Guide to the Show Caves of Britain* (Aylesbury: Shire, 1972)

Orme, B., *Anthropology for Archaeologists* (London: Duckworth, 1981)

Ousby, Ian (ed.), *James Plumptre's Britain: The Journals of a Tourist in the 1790s* (London: Hutchinson, 1992)

Paas, Frederick, *The Arch-Druid: An Historical Poem* (Sidmouth: [n.pub.], 1830), 4

Piggott, Stuart, *Ancient Britain and the Antiquarian Imagination: Ideas from the Renaissance to the Regency* (London: Thames and Hudson, 1989)

Polwhele, Richard, *The History of Devonshire*, Vol. I (London: Cadell and Davies, 1793)

Poulton-Smith, Anthony, *Ley Lines Across the Midlands* (Stroud: The History Press, 2009)

Pryor, Francis, *Britain AD: A Quest for Arthur, England and the Anglo-Saxons* (London: Harper Collins, 2004),

Richardson, R. C., 'William Camden and the Re-Discovery of England', *Transactions of the Leicestershire Archaeological and Historical Society* 78 (2004), 108–123

Russell, Ronald, *Lost Canals and Waterways of Britain* (London: Sphere, 1983)

Smiles, Sam, *The Image of Antiquity: Ancient Britain and the Romantic Imagination* (New Haven and London: Yale University Press, 1994)

Smith, Stephen, *Underground England: Travels Beneath our Cities and Country* (London: Little Brown, 2009)

Squires, Roger, *Britain's Restored Canals* (Ashbourne: Landmark, 2008)

Stout, Adam, *Creating Prehistory: Druids, Ley Hunters and Archaeologists in Pre-War Britain* (Oxford: Blackwell, 2008)

Street, Christopher, *London's Leylines: Pathways of Enlightenment* (London: Hermitage, 2011)

Stukeley, William, *Abury: A Temple of the British Druids* (London: W. Innys and R. Manby, 1743)
    Stonehenge: A Temple Restor'd to the British Druids (London: W. Innys and R. Manby, 1740)

Taylor, T., *The Prehistory of Sex* (London: Fourth Estate, 1996).

Timpson, John, *Timpson's Leylines: A Layman Tracking the Leys* (London: Cassell, 2001)

Watkins, Alfred, *Early British Trackways, Moats, Mounds, Camps and Sites: A Lecture* (London: Simpkin, Marshall and Co., 1922)
    The Ley Hunter's Manual: A Guide to Early Tracks (London: Simpkin, Marshall and Co., 1927)
    The Old Straight Track (London: Abacus, 1998 [1925])

Williamson, Tom, and Liz Bellamy, *Ley Lines in Question* (Tadworth: World's Work, 1983)

Wilton-Jones, Tarquin, *Ten Years in the Dark* (2002), www.cavinguk.co.uk/book/index.php

Wordsworth, William, 'Guilt and Sorrow: Or, Incidents Upon Salisbury

Plain', in John O'Hayden (ed.), *William Wordsworth: The Poems*, Vol. I (Harmondsworth: Penguin, 1977)

Worthington, Andy, *Stonehenge: Celebration and Subversion* (Loughborough: Alternative Albion, 2004)

Acknowledgements

Books and babies can be a tricky combination. Both of my daughters were born while this book was being written and so it really would never have been completed without the help, patience, and support of a whole team of people – first and foremost my parents Rosemary and Leonard Parker and my husband Nick Groom, but also Fiona Aylen, Karen Longworth, Katie Marchant and Helen and Mike Parker-Bray. My thanks must also go to my editors Dan Franklin and Clare Bullock at Jonathan Cape for their enthusiasm, advice, and guidance, to Jane Selley for copy-editing the manuscript, and to Darren Bennett for producing the maps. The book would never have got as far as Jonathan Cape without the wisdom and understanding of my agent David Godwin. And I would also like to thank Angus MacKinnon for his belief in the book in its early stages; Ronald Hutton for teaching me to write books rather than 'monographs'; and Mark Hurst for first taking me into caves and in search of megaliths. Thanks are due also to Chris Chapman and Adam Stout for generously sharing pictures, and to Alex Hill and the staff at Exeter University's Special Collections for help with sourcing and reproducing images. Finally, this book would have been impossible without the generous contributions of an array of amazing individuals who have unstintingly shared their stories, beliefs, and views of Britain: Graham Appleton, Andy Burnham, Philip Carr-Gomm, John Christian, Sue Day, Richard Fox, Grahame Gardner, Peter Gill, Roger Hanbury,

Robin Higgs, Brian Hope, Chris Jewell, Mickey Kaye, Dave Nixon, Eric Sargeant, Roger Squires, Christopher Street, John Stewart, Andy Walsh and Tarquin Wilton-Jones. To you all – this book is as much yours as it is mine.

Index